DEVELOPMENT

IN PRACTICE

Priorities and Strategies
for Education

Priorities and Strategies
for Education

A World Bank Review

THE WORLD BANK
WASHINGTON, D. C.

The Development in Practice series publishes reviews of the World
Bank's activities in different regions and sectors. It lays particular
emphasis on the progress that is being made and on the policies and
practices that hold the most promise of success in the effort to reduce
poverty in the developing world.

This report is a study by the World Bank's staff, and the judgments
made herein do not necessarily reflect the views of the Board of Executive
Directors or of the governments they represent.

Cover photo of schoolgirls in Fatehpur Sikri, India, by Maurice Asseo.

Library of Congress Cataloging-in-Publication Data

Priorities and strategies in education : a World Bank review.
    p.   cm. — (Development in practice)
   Includes bibliographical references   (p.   ).
   ISBN 0-8213-3311-9
   1. Education—Developing countries.   2. Education—Developing
countries—Finance.   3. Education, Secondary—Developing countries.
4. Education and state—Developing countries.   5. Educational
equalization—Developing countries.   6. Economic development—Effect
of education on.   I. International Bank for Reconstruction and
Development.   II. Series: Development in practice (Washington, D.C.)
LC2605.P756   1995
370'.9172'4—dc20   95-18770
                                                         CIP

Contents

v

FIGURES

BOXES

Foreword

EDUCATION produces knowledge, skills, values, and attitudes. It is essential for civic order and citizenship and for sustained economic growth and the reduction of poverty. Education is also about culture; it is the main instrument for disseminating the accomplishments of human civilization. These multiple purposes make education a key area of public policy in all countries. Its importance is recognized in several international conventions and in many national constitutions. In 1990 it was the subject of a landmark international meeting: the World Conference on Education for All, held in Jomtien, Thailand, under the joint sponsorship of the United Nations Development Programme (UNDP), the United Nations Educational, Scientific, and Cultural Organization (UNESCO), the United Nations Children's Fund (UNICEF), and the World Bank.

The civic purpose of education—the sharing of values throughout society—is becoming more salient in light of the widespread political liberalization of the past decade. This trend, which is most notable in Eastern Europe and Central Asia, also includes the consolidation of civilian democratic rule in Latin America, the introduction of multiparty systems in Africa, and the devolution of political power to subnational levels of government in many regions of the world.

Research and experience have also led to a deeper understanding of how education contributes to economic growth, the reduction of poverty, and the good governance essential for implementing sound economic and social policies. In line with these changing circumstances and perceptions, the World Bank's financing of education has grown rapidly in the past fifteen years, and the Bank is now the single largest source of external finance for education in low- and middle-income countries. Projects to support primary and lower-secondary education—basic education—have become increasingly prominent in Bank lending for the sector. This emphasis is in harmony with the recommendations of the World Conference on Education for All.

The expansion of World Bank lending for education has been accompanied by a series of studies on education policy in developing countries: *Education in Sub-Saharan Africa* (1988), *Primary Education* (1990), *Vocational and Technical Education and Training* (1991), and *Higher Education* (1994). In addition, recent *World Development Reports—Poverty* (1990), *The Challenge of Development* (1991), *Investing in Health* (1993), and *Workers in an Integrating World* (1995)—have highlighted the importance of education for development.

This Development in Practice book—the first overall review of education by the World Bank since the 1980 sector policy paper—synthesizes the findings of the publications issued in the intervening years, adds a review of secondary education, reflecting the results of ongoing work in the Bank's Human Development Department, and extends these results into the areas of sectoral finance and management. It also draws heavily on UNESCO's *World Education Report* (1993). The report outlines policy options that low- and middle-income countries can adopt to meet educational challenges as they move toward the twenty-first century. It is designed to assist policymakers in these countries, especially those concerned with the education system as a whole and with the allocation of public resources to education. It is also intended for World Bank staff who work with client countries to support education policies and projects.

The report discusses policy options in education, not the details of education projects. It focuses on the formal education system and the role that governments can play through sound financial and managerial policies that encourage the expansion of the private sector and improvement in the functioning of public institutions. It does not pretend to be exhaustive; for example, it does not discuss in-depth training (covered in the 1991 paper) or adult education, which is in the current work program of the Human Development Department.

What the report does do is to treat the mainstream formal education sector as a whole. It focuses on the contribution of formal education to sustained economic growth and the reduction of poverty. It emphasizes approaches and ways of determining priorities and strategies, recognizing that policies must be tailored to each country according to its stage of educational and economic development and its historical and political context. Throughout, it keeps in view the World Bank's fundamental objective, which guides the Bank's work in education as in every sector: helping borrowers reduce poverty and improve living standards through sustainable growth and investment in people.

Armeane M. Choksi
Vice President
Human Capital Development and Operations Policy
The World Bank

Acknowledgments

THIS report was prepared by a team led by Nicholas Burnett and consisting of Tom Eisemon, Kari Marble, and Harry Anthony Patrinos, under the general direction of K. Y. Amoako and the immediate supervision of Peter R. Moock in the Education and Social Policy Department. Other major contributors to the report were Arun Joshi, Marlaine Lockheed and Kin Bing Wu; material was also provided by Barbara Bruns, Sarbani Chakraborty, Helen Craig, Joy Del Rosso, Reed Garfield, Indermit Gill, Masooma Habib, Jane Hannaway, Ward Heneveld, Donald Holsinger, Theresa Moran, Christina Rawley, Omporn Regel, Rajendra Swamy and Stella Tamayo. Helpful comments on earlier drafts were given by Arvil Van Adams, Jean-Claude Eicher, Vincent Greaney, Lauritz Holm-Nielsen, Bruno Laporte, Jon Lauglo, Michael Mertaugh, John Middleton, Alain Mingat, Paud Murphy, François Orivel, Jamil Salmi, Nate Scovronick, Lyn Squire, Jee-Peng Tan, Zafiris Tzannatos, Michael Walton, Maureen Woodhall, and Adrian Ziderman. Members of a Bankwide advisory panel that provided valuable assistance were Mark Baird, Carl Dahlman, Birger Fredriksen, Wadi Haddad, Ralph Harbison, Roslyn Hees, Stephen Heyneman, Emmanuel Jimenez, Homi Kharas, Jack Maas, Himelda Martinez, Philip Musgrove, George Psacharopoulos, Julian Schweitzer, Richard Skolnik, James Socknat and Donald Winkler. The paper was reviewed in September 1994 by an external panel consisting of ministers, senior officials, and academics from Armenia, Colombia, France, Guinea, India, Japan, Jordan, Mexico, Nigeria, Pakistan, the Philippines, the Russian Federation, the Slovak Republic, Thailand, Uganda, and the United Kingdom. Discussions were also held with staff members of the Organisation for Economic Co-operation and Development (OECD), UNESCO, UNICEF, the Canadian International Development Agency (CIDA); the Swedish International Development Authority (SIDA), and the U.S. Agency for International Development (USAID); with the UNESCO Commission on Education for the Twenty-First Century, chaired by Jacques Delors; with donor agency representatives meeting under the auspices of the International Working Group on Education; with the Commonwealth Ministers of Education; with British academics and officials at a meeting organized by the British Council; and with Education International. Jo Bischoff, Ian Conachy, Richard Crum, Kari Labrie, and Margot Verbeeck helped prepare drafts of the report.

Definitions and Data Notes

FOR ITS operational purposes, the World Bank groups low- and middle-income countries (as defined by the Bank's International Economics Department) into six regions: Sub-Saharan Africa, East Asia and the Pacific, Europe and Central Asia, Latin America and the Caribbean, the Middle East and North Africa, and South Asia. The analysis in this report uses these regions and, for some comparisons, two other groups: all low- and middle-income countries, and the members of the Organisation for Economic Co-operation and Development (OECD).

Because of gaps in data availability, some regional averages for Europe and Central Asia do not include the countries of the former Soviet Union.

Unless otherwise stated, dollar amounts are current U.S. dollars. A billion is a thousand million.

Summary

EDUCATION is critical for economic growth and poverty reduction. Changing technology and economic reforms are creating dramatic shifts in the structure of economies, industries, and labor markets throughout the world. The rapid increase in knowledge and the pace of changing technology raise the possibility of sustained economic growth with more frequent job changes during individuals' lives. These developments have created two key priorities for education: it must meet economies' growing demands for adaptable workers who can readily acquire new skills, and it must support the continued expansion of knowledge. This paper synthesizes World Bank work on education since publication of the last sector policy paper, in 1980, and considers options for the Bank's borrowing countries.

The World Bank's strategy for reducing poverty focuses on promoting the productive use of labor—the main asset of the poor—and providing basic social services to the poor. Investment in education contributes to the accumulation of human capital, which is essential for higher incomes and sustained economic growth. Education—especially basic (primary and lower-secondary) education—helps reduce poverty by increasing the productivity of the poor, by reducing fertility and improving health, and by equipping people with the skills they need to participate fully in the economy and in society. More generally, education helps strengthen civil institutions and build national capacity and good governance—critical elements in the implementation of sound economic and social policies.

Basic education encompasses general skills such as language, science and mathematics, and communications that provide the foundation for further education and training. It also includes the development of attitudes necessary for the workplace. Academic and vocational skills are imparted at higher levels; on-the-job training and work-related continuing education update those skills.

Progress and Challenges

The economies of low- and middle-income countries have been growing at historically rapid rates. Progress in education—expanded enrollments and longer schooling—has contributed to this growth and so has helped to reduce poverty in developing countries. In 1990 a typical 6-year-old child in a developing country could expect to attend school for 8.5 years, up from 7.6 years in 1980. In Eastern Europe and Central Asia schooling for nine to ten years is the rule; in East Asia and in Latin America and the Caribbean primary education is almost universal. Countries in the Middle East and North Africa are making steady progress; so are those in South Asia, although they have a considerable distance to go. Sub-Saharan Africa is lagging; certain countries are making gains, but overall, primary enrollment ratios are actually declining.

Yet despite these substantial achievements in the world as a whole, major challenges remain: to increase access to education in some countries, to improve equity, to improve quality, and, where needed, to speed educational reform.

Access

If the current high population growth rates in Africa, South Asia, and the Middle East and North Africa continue, the number of 6-to-11-year-old children not in school will increase to 162 million by 2015, from 129 million in 1990. To make matters worse, only two-thirds of children who start primary school complete it. As a result, adult illiteracy, which already affects over 900 million people, most of them women, is likely to remain a major problem.

In most countries, more children wish to go to secondary school than are able to enroll, and the demand for higher education is in general increasing faster than the supply. The enrollment gap between the transition economies of Europe and Central Asia and the members of the Organisation for Economic Co-operation and Development (OECD) is also widening as enrollment ratios decline in the former and rise in the OECD countries.

Equity

The issue of equity mainly affects several overlapping disadvantaged groups, including the poor, linguistic and ethnic minorities, nomads, refugees, and street and working children. The different access that boys and girls have to the education system in some parts of the world is also very important because it contributes to gender differences later in life. The gender gap in expected years of schooling is now very small in most countries in Europe and Central Asia and in Latin America. It remains large in the Middle East and North Africa and in South Asia, where it is not closing at all.

Quality

The quality of education is poor at all levels in low- and middle-income countries. Students in developing countries have a mean level of achievement below that in industrial countries, and their performance shows a much greater variation around the mean.

Speeding up Reform

Delays in reforming education systems to keep pace with economic structures are most apparent in the transition economies of Eastern and Central Europe. Lags in reform can hinder growth; conversely, timely reform can pay off in terms of economic growth and poverty reduction, as evidenced by the East Asian countries that have generally invested heavily in basic human capital, both male and female.

Finance and Management

Present systems for financing and managing education are often inappropriate for meeting the challenges discussed above. Public financing, moreover, is growing more difficult as enrollments expand.

Public intervention in education can be justified on several counts: it can reduce inequality, open opportunities for the poor and disadvantaged, compensate for market failures in lending for education, and make information about the benefits and availability of education generally available. But public spending on education is often inefficient and inequitable. It is inefficient when it is misallocated among uses; it is inequitable when qualified potential students are unable to enroll in institutions because educational opportunities are lacking or because of inability to pay.

Basic education ought to be the priority for public spending on education in those countries that have yet to achieve near-universal enrollment at the primary and lower-secondary levels. Most countries are already allocating the highest share of public spending on education to primary education. Subsidies increase the demand for higher education. Although public spending per student in higher education is falling in comparison with that per primary student, it remains very high. In Africa, for instance, spending per student in higher education is about forty-four times that per student in primary education, and the share of higher education in total public spending on education is now higher than in any other region of the world. Yet one-half of Africa's primary-school-age children are not enrolled in school, and universities in the region are often of low quality.

Inefficient mixes of inputs—for example, between staff and instructional materials—can contribute to low learning achievement and high repetition and dropout rates. For effective learning, the input mix must vary from country to country and school to school according to local conditions. International comparisons and interschool comparisons can, however, provide broad guidance. Modest increases in student-teacher ratios tend to improve education when they permit resources to be reallocated to other critical inputs, such as textbooks. School buildings can be built more cheaply than is usually the case at present, and they will last longer if adequate maintenance funding is ensured. Consolidation of small schools and the use of multigrade teaching and multiple shifts offer other possibilities for using buildings more efficiently.

Public spending on primary education generally favors the poor, but public spending on education as a whole often favors the affluent because of the heavy subsidization of the upper-secondary and higher education levels, which usually have relatively few students from poor families. Public sector spending for higher education is particularly inequitable because the subsidy per student is higher than that for basic education, even though higher education students come disproportionately from richer families.

The Potential for Saving through Efficiency

In 1990 public spending on education equaled 5.2 percent of gross national product (GNP) in the Middle East and North Africa but only 3.4 percent in East Asia. Yet in both regions an average 6-year-old child could expect to complete more than nine years of school. Public spending on education in Africa, which has the lowest enrollment ratios of any region, represents a greater share of GNP (4.2 percent) than in Latin America (3.7 percent) or East Asia, which have largely achieved universal primary education. Some countries that spend very little on education could dramatically improve results simply by increasing public spending. In many countries, however, improved education could be achieved with the same or even less public spending by focusing public spending on the lower levels of education and increasing internal efficiency, as has been done in East Asia.

The Need for New Sources of Finance

The inefficiencies and inequities described above, along with expanding enrollments in public schools at all levels, have contributed to increasing the share of GNP devoted to public spending on education. The result is increasing pressure on public funds at the same time that many countries, especially in Eastern Europe and Africa, are experiencing general fiscal difficulties. During the 1980s public spending on education as a share of GNP remained stable or increased, and its share of total central government spending increased, in nearly every region of the developing world. In Latin America, which experienced debt-induced recession, real public expenditure per primary student fell. In Africa real spending per student decreased at both the primary and the secondary levels. Real spending per student in higher education fell in all regions. As enrollments increase, resources per student decline, and so will the quality of schooling, unless public spending becomes more efficient.

Although measures to increase the efficiency of public spending on education can make existing funds more productive, such measures alone may not be enough. Some countries have chosen to reallocate public spending to education from other publicly funded activities, such as defense and inefficient public enterprises that can be run better by the private sector. Other countries have found a way, within their macroeconomic policies, to increase the revenues of government and thereby have more to spend on education. Yet others have sought to supplement public funds for education with private funds.

Private financing can be encouraged either to fund private institutions or to supplement the income of publicly funded institutions. Some countries prohibit private schools and universities; others regulate them excessively. Since private schools are usually financed through fees, such restrictions crowd out private spending on education that would otherwise have occurred and so increase the pressure on publicly funded schools. Another argument for private schools and universities is that, even though they tend to draw their students from more advantaged socioeconomic backgrounds, they promote diversity and provide useful competition for public institutions, especially at the higher levels of education.

Charging fees for students at publicly funded institutions raises difficult questions concerning equity, access, and taxation. If all students attending public schools at all levels are charged, the poor will be hit particularly hard, discouraging their enrollment. Scholarship and other systems can be introduced to offset this problem, but they are complex to administer at lower levels of education. At the upper-secondary and higher levels, a much stronger case exists for payment of fees by students at public institutions. For these levels, the gap between the private and the social returns to education is generally much greater than in basic education. This inequity can be overcome by charging the student either from current family income or from future earnings, through a loan scheme or through the tax system.

Organizing Education for Effective Schooling

Most education systems are directly managed by central or state governments, which put a great deal of effort into dealing with such issues as teacher salary negotiations, school construction programs, and curriculum reform. This central management, extending even to instructional inputs and the classroom environment, allows little room for the flexibility that leads to effective learning.

The main ways in which governments can help improve the quality of education are setting standards, supporting inputs known to improve achievement, adopting flexible strategies for the acquisition and use of inputs, and monitoring performance. Generally, however, these steps are not taken because of the weight of existing education spending and management practices and the vested interests associated with them.

Standards

Governments can help improve academic achievement by setting clear and high performance standards in core subjects.

Inputs

Learning requires five inputs: the student's capacity and motivation to learn, the subject to be learned, a teacher who knows the subject and can teach it, time for learning, and tools for teaching and learning.

Capacity for learning can be increased through high-quality preschool educational programs and through preschool and school-based programs to remedy short-term hunger, protein-energy and micronutrient malnutrition, hearing and vision impairments, highly prevalent health conditions such as parasitic infections, and inappropriate health and nutrition practices. Such programs are even more effective when combined with efforts to improve the physical environment in the school.

The *curriculum* defines the subjects to be taught and furnishes general guidance on the frequency and duration of instruction. Curricula and syllabi should be closely tied to performance standards and measures of outcome. No single curriculum is appropriate for all or most developing countries, but some generalizations can be made. At the primary level curricula are fairly standard, but there are often too many subjects, reducing the time available for teaching core skills. The most effective initial language of instruction is the child's native language. At the secondary level curricula vary considerably, particularly in science education and vocational education. Science education, because of its importance for economic development, is increasingly integrated in curricula; specialized vocational and technical education, which yields much lower social returns than does general secondary education, is best conducted in the workplace, after a grounding in general education. Vocational education works best when the private sector is directly involved in its provision, financing, and governance. At all levels, making the curriculum gender-sensitive is particularly important for encouraging girls' education.

The most effective teachers appear to be those with good *knowledge of the subject* and a wide repertoire of teaching skills. The most effective strategy for ensuring that teachers have adequate subject knowledge is to recruit suitably educated teachers whose knowledge has been demonstrated through assessed performance. This strategy is followed for secondary and higher education teachers but is rare at the primary level. In-service training to improve teachers' subject knowledge and related pedagogical practices is most effective when it is linked directly to classroom practice and provided by the head teacher.

The amount of actual *time* devoted to learning is consistently related to achievement. Students in low- and middle-income countries receive fewer hours of classroom instruction than those in OECD countries—a consequence of a shorter official school year, unscheduled school closings, teacher and student absences, and miscellaneous disruptions. Instructional time can be increased by extending the official school year; by permitting flexible scheduling to accommodate the demands of agricultural seasons, religious holidays, and children's domestic chores; and by assigning homework.

The most effective *instructional materials* are blackboards, chalk, and textbooks. Supplementary reading material is particularly critical for improving reading skills.

Flexibility

Flexibility in combining and managing inputs and monitoring performance is vital for effective schooling. Yet many education systems in developing countries are still rigidly centralized; for instance, a central authority often selects and purchases textbooks and prescribes teaching methodology. School governing bodies, principals, and teachers, with their intimate knowledge of local conditions, are best able to select the most appropriate package of inputs. Under the right circumstances, making schools and higher education institutions accountable to parents, communities, and students helps bring about more effective learning and hence improves educational quality. Three conditions are necessary for this result: shared goals regarding the learning objectives of the school, professionalism on the part of teachers, and schools' autonomy in allocating instructional resources flexibly. A further promising approach is school-based leadership that ensures an effective climate for learning.

Priorities for Reform

Reforming education finance and management means redefining the role of government in six key ways, with the order of priority depending on country circumstances. Table 1 illustrates how these measures contribute to the goals of improving access, equity, and quality and overcoming delays in reform.

A Higher Priority for Education

Education is more important than ever for economic development and poverty reduction, and its role in this effort is better understood. Education, for girls as well as for boys, therefore deserves a higher priority on government agendas—not just those of ministries of education. This imperative has long been recognized in East Asia and is increasingly coming to be understood elsewhere, particularly Latin America. Other countries still need to give education more attention. Education alone will not reduce poverty; complementary macroeconomic policies and physical investments are also needed.

Attention to Outcomes

Educational priorities should be set with reference to outcomes, using economic analysis, standard setting, and measurement of achievement through learning assessments. An approach that looks at the whole sector is key for setting priorities; attention to only one level of education is insufficient. Economic analysis usually compares benefits (in labor productivity, as measured by wages) with costs, for individuals and for society. It identifies as priorities for public investment those investments for which the social rate of return is highest and the level of public subsidization is lowest. Rates of return must be calculated for specific country circumstances and cannot be assumed. Because

TABLE 1   CHALLENGES IN EDUCATION AND KEY REFORMS

Strategy	Access	Equity	Quality	Overcoming delays in reform
Higher priority for education	✓	✓	✓	✓
Attention to outcomes			✓	✓
Emphasis on basic education in public investment	✓	✓	✓	
Attention to equity		✓		
Household involvement	✓	✓	✓	
Autonomous institutions	✓		✓	

of the difficulty of valuing external benefits not reflected in wages, cost-benefit analysis should be applied with caution.

The high rates of return estimated for basic education in most developing countries strongly suggest that investments to improve enrollments and retention in basic education should generally have the highest priority in countries that have not yet achieved universal basic education. Some improvements in educational efficiency or quality will often be possible through policy changes that require no specific investments.

Decisions about public education priorities beyond basic education have to be taken within a broad sectoral approach and will vary according to country. Countries that have largely achieved universal primary and lower-secondary education are likely to consider upper-secondary and higher education the priorities, and they can often make informed decisions about these postcompulsory levels through the prudent use of economic analysis focused on labor market outcomes. It has been shown, for example, that the returns to general secondary education are much higher than those to highly specialized vocational secondary education, although analysis has not yet looked into the returns to investment in the more "general" type of vocational education that is now becoming prevalent in many OECD countries. Countries that have yet to achieve universal basic education will need to pay attention to all levels of education, using economic analysis to guide decisions about which investments will have the greatest effect. Focusing on outcomes also entails the establishment of performance standards, particularly for primary and general secondary schools, and development of a system of assessments to monitor what students are learning. Standards, curricula, and monitoring are most effective when they are directly linked through appropriate incentives.

Emphasis on Basic Education in Public Investment

A more efficient, equitable, and sustainable allocation of new public invest-ment on education would do much to meet the challenges that education sys-tems face today. Efficiency is achieved by making public investments where they will yield the highest returns—usually, for education investments, in basic education. To achieve equity, the government needs to ensure that no qualified student is denied access to education because of inability to pay. Because the gap between private and social returns is larger for higher education than for basic education, students and parents may well be willing to bear part of the costs of higher education. Governments can also encourage private financing by taking on some of the risk that makes financial institutions reluctant to lend for higher education.

A policy package of fees and efficient expenditure in the public sector might consist of:

■ Free basic education, including cost-sharing with communities and targeted stipends for children from poor households

■ Selective charging of fees for upper-secondary education, combined with targeted scholarships

■ Fees for all public higher education, combined with loans, taxes, and other schemes to allow needy students to defer payment until they become income-earners, and a targeted scholarship scheme to overcome the reluctance of the poor to accumulate debt against uncertain future earnings

■ Assurance of quality primary education for all children by making that level the top priority for public spending on education in all countries

■ Improved access to quality general secondary education (initially lower-secondary and later all levels of secondary) as the second priority, once all children are receiving good primary education

■ Efficient public spending at the school and institution level.

Fiscal sustainability also requires the continuous projection of the implications of public expenditure and consistent efforts to ensure that financing plans and mechanisms are in place.

Attention to Equity

Equity has two principal aspects: (a) everyone's right to a basic education—the basic knowledge and skills necessary to function effectively in society—and

(b) the government's obligation to ensure that qualified potential students are not denied education because they are poor or female, are from disadvantaged ethnic minorities or geographically remote regions, or have special educational needs. At the lowest and compulsory levels of education, equity simply means ensuring that schools are available. Beyond that, it means having fair and valid ways of determining potential students' qualifications for entry.

Achieving equity requires both financial and administrative measures. Financial measures, such as scholarships, are important at all levels to enable the poor to gain an education. Scholarships can cover fees and other direct costs, such as transport and uniforms and, when appropriate, can compensate families for the indirect costs of sending children to school—for example, loss of labor services for the household. Administrative measures can increase enrollments of the poor, females, linguistic minorities, and students with special educational needs. Programs designed to demonstrate the importance of educating children can increase the demand for schooling among the poor. Measures to encourage schooling for girls can include setting aside all-girl classrooms and schools, locating schools within easy access of girls' homes, providing separate sanitary facilities, constructing boundary walls, increasing the number of female teachers, providing childcare centers, and adjusting school hours to accommodate girls' work at home. For linguistic minorities, bilingual programs and schools offering a choice of language of instruction are important, especially in primary education. Special programs, such as deworming and micronutrient supplementation, to improve the nutrition and health of schoolchildren can reduce the number of children with physical and learning disabilities. The (usually low) costs of educating children with minor impairments can often be shared with nongovernmental organizations.

Household Involvement

Around the world, parents and communities are becoming more involved in the governance of their children's schools. Effective involvement in school governance does not come easily, however, and training is generally advisable.

Several countries have a long tradition of parental choice. Increased experimentation with school choice is another recent educational reform, particularly in OECD countries. There is as yet no evidence that competition among schools either improves or worsens school performance.

For choice to be effective, the student must have more than one possible school. The institutions should have some distinguishing characteristics—for example, in what aspects of the curriculum are emphasized, in teaching styles, and, at higher levels, in course offerings. Finally, institutions need to enjoy considerable autonomy in how they teach. The availability of a variety of institutions enables parents and students to exercise choice and thus gives institutions an incentive to adapt to demand.

Increased household involvement carries major risks:

■ Implementation of systemwide education policies can be more difficult.

■ Enforcement of broader national objectives can be hampered.

■ Social segregation may increase if schools become polarized between elite academies and schools for the children of the poor and uneducated.

■ Equity may be reduced if schools and institutions accept students on the basis of their ability to pay rather than on academic entrance qualifications.

■ Parents may lack the information they need to make judgments about quality.

The first four risks can be mitigated relatively easily through policies for the provision of public funding. Such funds can be made available only to schools that follow certain practices, can be higher per student for poor children, and can be accompanied by restrictions on fee levels. The fifth risk can be reduced through government efforts to provide open and independent information about school quality.

Autonomous Institutions

The quality of education can benefit when schools have the autonomy to use instructional inputs according to local school and community conditions and are accountable to parents and communities. Fully autonomous institutions have authority to allocate their resources (not necessarily to raise them), and they are able to create an educational environment adapted to local conditions inside and outside the school. There is still little evidence about the impact of increased school-level flexibility on the overall quality of education systems in developing countries. As with school choice, therefore, some caution is called for as more countries experiment with increased school autonomy.

Accountable autonomous institutions can be encouraged by both administrative and financial means. Administrative measures include giving school management the authority to allocate resources—for example, the authority to deploy personnel and to alter such things as the timing of the school day and year and the language of instruction to fit local conditions. Most critically, teachers need to have the authority to determine classroom practices, within limits set by a broad national curriculum.

Financial measures to encourage school and institutional autonomy and accountability can include:

- The use of local and central government taxation

- Cost-sharing with local communities

- The allocation of block grants to communities and schools without restrictions on the allocation of the funds

- Fee charging at higher levels of education

- Encouragement of revenue diversification

- The use of financing mechanisms in which money follows students, such as capitation grants, vouchers and student loans

- Funding based on output and quality.

Reliance on local funding must be tempered with adjustments by higher levels of government to compensate for differing resource levels among localities. Local control of resources need not imply local raising of revenues. The goal of local financing of schools should be to improve learning, not to reduce overall resources.

The main risks of school autonomy are the creation of inequalities in educational opportunities and failure to adhere to the national standards and curriculum. These risks can be largely mitigated by clearly distinguishing school-level management and resource allocation from exclusive reliance on local financing and by handling performance standards, curricula, and learning assessments at the national or regional level. There are few risks to increased institutional autonomy in higher education.

Implementing Change

The relative priority accorded each reform depends on specific country circumstances. A sectoral approach—one that considers the efficiency, equity, and quality of the education sector as a whole and gives due attention to the larger policy environment and institution building—is essential.

In all countries entrenched ways of operating and vested interests will make change difficult. Education is intensely political: it affects the majority of citizens, involves all levels of government, almost always makes up the single largest component of public spending in developing countries, and involves public subsidies that are biased in favor of the elite. Prevailing systems of education spending and management often protect the interests of teachers' unions, university students, elites, and the central government rather than those of parents, communities, and the poor. There are, however, strategies that can ease change. Financing and management reforms are best introduced in parallel with the *expansion of educational opportunities*. Sometimes the change itself makes for expansion—for example, when prohibitions on the private sector are lifted. Increased cost-sharing in public higher education is politically most feasible when it is linked to expansion of opportunities for higher education. *Building national consensus* involves stakeholders in the education system in national consultation mechanisms. *Increasing the involvement of parents and communities* by making schools autonomous and accountable can offset the power of vested interests; it is also critical for increasing flexibility and improving instructional quality. *Careful design of reform measures* is necessary to avoid disrupting the vital links among education subsectors. An essential, although often neglected, step is the provision of appropriate resources and mechanisms to accompany policy changes.

The transition economies of Eastern and Central Europe have high primary and secondary enrollment ratios but need to adjust the entire education system toward the needs of a market economy. It is particularly important for these countries to maintain funding levels for basic and upper-secondary education, to shift away from overspecialization at vocational, technical, and higher education institutions, and to reform the governance and financing of higher education.

The World Bank and Education

The World Bank made its first loan for education in 1963, and the Bank is now the largest single source of external financing for education in developing countries. Since 1980 the total volume of lending for education has tripled, and its share in overall Bank lending has doubled. Primary and secondary education are increasingly important; in fiscal 1990–94 these levels represented half of all Bank lending for education. Early Bank lending for education concentrated on Africa, East Asia, and the Middle East, but today lending is significant in all regions. Girls' education is at the forefront, and increasing attention is being given to the educational needs of ethnic minorities and indigenous people. Today Bank funds are used less for buildings and more for other educational inputs. The narrow project focus of the past is increasingly giving way to a broad sectoral approach.

The World Bank is strongly committed to continued support for education. However, even though Bank funding now accounts for about a quarter of all aid to education, this funding still represents only about 0.5 percent of developing countries' total spending on the sector. Thus, the World Bank's main contribution must be advice, designed to help governments develop education policies suitable for the circumstances of their countries. Bank financing will generally be designed to leverage spending and policy change by national authorities. Future operations will therefore adopt an even more explicit sectorwide policy focus in order to support changes in educational financing and management. Because of the need to consult key stakeholders, this strategy may increase both the resources and the time needed to prepare projects. In increasingly decentralized contexts, the stakeholders will include not only central governments but also other levels of government, as well as communities, parents, teachers, and employers. Donor cooperation will extend to broad policy advice, as well as investment coordination.

Bank programs will encourage governments to give a higher priority to education and educational reform, particularly as economic reform takes hold as a permanent process. Projects will take more account of outcomes and their relation to inputs, making explicit use of cost-benefit analysis, participatory methods, learning assessments, and improved monitoring and evaluation. The share of basic education in total Bank lending for education is expected to continue to increase, especially in the poorest countries, which receive International Development Association (IDA) funds. This emphasis will be embedded in a sectoral approach that recognizes the importance of the various parts of the education system, the interdependencies among these parts, and the need to base both the emphasis and the nature of Bank assistance on a determination of where the Bank can be most useful in the particular circumstances of each country.

Bank-supported projects will pay greater attention to equity—especially education for girls, for disadvantaged ethnic minorities, and for the poor—and consequently to early childhood education. Projects will support household involvement in school governance and in school choice through an increased emphasis on the regulatory framework for education, on quality-enhancing mechanisms such as outcome monitoring and inspection, on recurrent cost financing, and on demand-side financing mechanisms such as targeted scholarships for the poor, stipends for girls, and student loan schemes for higher education. They will encourage flexible management of instructional resources, complemented by national assessment and examination systems to provide incentives. In all these areas, Bank-supported projects will focus more intently on institutional development—including strengthening educational administration—and appropriate financial mechanisms, and the Bank's staff will pay increased attention to implementation.

Basic education will continue to receive the highest priority in the Bank's education lending to countries that have not yet achieved universal literacy and adequate access, equity, and quality at that level. The Bank's sectoral approach means that in countries that have yet to achieve universal literacy, its involvement in higher education will continue to concentrate mainly on making the financing of this level more equitable and cost-effective so that primary and secondary education can receive increased attention at the margin.

As the basic education system develops in coverage and effectiveness, more attention can be devoted to the upper-secondary and higher levels. Bank lending for higher education will support countries' efforts to adopt policy reforms that will allow the subsector to operate more efficiently and at lower public cost. Countries prepared to adopt a higher education policy framework that stresses a differentiated institutional structure and diversified resource base, with greater emphasis on private providers and private funding, will continue to receive priority.

PART I

The Record of Experience and the Tasks Ahead

EDUCATION—in particular, primary and lower-secondary education—is critical for economic growth and reduction of poverty, especially at a time when, as a result of technological change and economic reform, labor market structures are shifting dramatically. The spread of education has reduced poverty by helping developing countries' economies grow at historically rapid rates. Yet major challenges remain: to expand access in some countries and, in many others, to increase equity, improve educational quality, and speed educational reform. The current systems of finance and management are frequently not well suited to meeting these challenges. Public spending on education is too often inefficient and inequitable. In view of the competition for and pressure on public funds, new sources of financing are needed. And changes may be needed in the organization and management of education systems to permit the flexibility and choice that contribute to better student achievement and prospects. The next four chapters examine how education contributes to economic development and what actions are needed to meet the demands of a changing world and workplace.

CHAPTER ONE

Education and Development

EDUCATION is a major instrument for economic and social development. It is central to the World Bank's strategy for helping countries reduce poverty and improve living standards through sustainable growth and investment in people. This twofold strategy calls for promoting the productive use of labor—the principal asset of the poor—and providing basic social services to the poor (World Bank 1990b).

Investment in education leads to the accumulation of human capital, which is key to sustained economic growth and increasing incomes. Education, especially basic (primary and lower-secondary) education, also contributes to poverty reduction by increasing the productivity of the poor's labor, by reducing fertility and improving health, and by equipping people to participate fully in the economy and in society. In addition, education contributes to the strengthening of the institutions of civil society, to national capacity building, and to good governance, all of which are increasingly recognized as critical elements in the effective implementation of sound economic and social policies.

Education and Economic Growth

Education contributes to economic growth, but by itself it will not generate growth. The strongest growth comes about when investment in both human and physical capital takes place in economies with competitive markets for goods and factors of production. Such markets are the product of macroeconomic stability, well-functioning labor markets, and an openness to international trade and flows of technology.

Economic growth is explained only in part by stocks of labor and physical capital. A large component of growth stems from improvements in the quality of the labor force, including increased education and better health, together with technological progress and economies of scale (T. W. Schultz 1961; Denison 1967; World Bank 1991d). New theories of economic growth suggest that faster technological change increases the long-run economic growth rate. Technological change increases faster, in turn, when workers are more highly educated. Thus, the accumulation of human capital, and specifically of knowledge, facilitates the development of new technologies and is a source of self-sustaining growth (Romer 1986; Lucas 1988; Azariadis and Drazen 1990; Barro 1991).

Education contributes to economic growth both through the increased individual productivity brought about by the acquisition of skills and attitudes and through the accumulation of knowledge. The contribution of education can be estimated by its impact on productivity, measured by comparing the difference

---

BOX 1.1   RATES OF RETURN TO EDUCATION

The concept of the rate of return to investment in education is very similar to that for any other investment project: it is a summary of the costs and benefits of the investment that apply at different points in time, and it is expressed in an annual (percentage) yield, similar to that quoted for bank savings accounts or government bonds. If the rate of return to education is 10 percent, this means that when $100,000 is invested in education, there will be an annual benefit of $10,000 over the lifetime of the average graduate, over and above what the same person would have earned without the investment.

Assume that an 18-year-old secondary-school graduate is driven only by monetary considerations on whether to "invest" in a four-year university degree. The prospective student has to compare the costs and benefits associated with going to college. The direct cost is $10,000 a year for tuition and other expenses related to study. In addition, the student would incur an indirect (or opportunity) cost because of not being able to work while attending college. This is approximated by what 18-to-21-year-olds with a secondary-school leaving certificate earn in the labor market—say, $20,000 a year. On the benefits side, the student expects to be making, on average, approximately $15,000 a year more in the future than a secondary-school graduate would over his or her lifetime.

A rough way of summarizing these costs and benefits is to divide the annual benefit of $15,000 by the lump-sum cost of $120,000, yielding a 12.5

in earnings over time of individuals with and without a particular course of education and the cost to the economy of producing that education. This measure is known as the social rate of return to investing in education, although it does not capture all social benefits or all external effects (box 1.1). Rates of return to education can be difficult to measure in some cases (Weale 1993)—though no more so than for other sectors such as agriculture and transport—but they have withstood the tests of more than three decades of careful scrutiny (T. P. Schultz 1994). And, as was concluded almost two decades ago, human capital theory has no genuine rival of equal breadth and rigor (Blaug 1976).

Rates of return to education are very high in low- and middle-income countries (table 1.1). Country circumstances differ, but, in general, in economies with less than universal basic education, rates of return are greatest for primary education, followed by secondary and then higher education. Interestingly, economies with universal primary education that have undergone rapid growth tend to show a higher rate of return to secondary than to primary education (Jain 1991; T. P. Schultz 1993, 1994).

---

percent rate of return to investment in higher education. The logic of this calculation is similar to that of buying a $120,000 bond with a annual coupon of $15,000. The yield of the bond is 12.5 percent.

The example given above refers to a private rate of return, where the costs are what the individual actually pays in order to receive an education. A social rate of return calculation includes on the cost side the full resource cost of one's education—that is, not only what the individual pays but also what it really costs society to educate one person. Since in most countries education is heavily subsidized, the social cost is much higher than the private cost. Hence a social rate of return is typically less than the corresponding private rate of return.

Beyond these monetary adjustments, the social rate of return should ideally include the externalities, or spillover benefits, associated with education. One of the main arguments used to justify public subsidy of education has to do with externalities, which affect society as a whole but are not captured by the individual. Since the social benefits of education exceed the private benefits, governments subsidize education to prevent underinvestment.

As in most other sectors, externalities are extremely difficult to measure and are not reflected in earnings. Social rates of return, as conventionally computed on the basis of monetary earnings and costs, thus underestimate the true social returns to investment in education. If one could include externalities, social rates of return might well be higher than private rates of return to education.

TABLE 1.1   RATES OF RETURN TO INVESTMENT IN EDUCATION BY REGION AND LEVEL
OF SCHOOLING

| | *Social* | | | *Private* | | |
Region	Primary	Secondary	Higher	Primary	Secondary	Higher
Low- and middle-income countries						
Sub-Saharan Africa	24.3	18.2	11.2	41.3	26.6	27.8
Asia	19.9	13.3	11.7	39.0	18.9	19.9
Europe, Middle East, and North Africa	15.5	11.2	10.6	17.4	15.9	21.7
Latin America and the Caribbean	17.9	12.8	12.3	26.2	16.8	19.7
OECD countries	n.a.	10.2	8.7	n.a.	12.4	12.3

n.a. Not applicable.
Source: Psacharopoulos 1994.

In almost all countries, rates of return to investment in all levels of education exceed the long-run opportunity cost of capital (usually estimated at 8–10 percent in real terms), making education an excellent investment. Caution, it should be noted, is necessary when looking at rates of return. They can be misleading when, for instance, labor markets are heavily regulated and earnings do not reflect marginal productivity.

Recent studies confirm the importance of education, and especially primary education, for growth. Cross-country studies suggest the possibility of a threshold level of human capital accumulation beyond which a country's growth may accelerate (Azariadis and Drazen 1990; Lau, Jamison, and Louat 1991). This concept is essentially a reconfirmation of the original hypothesis that formalized a threshold-type relationship between human capital and economic growth (Bowman and Anderson 1963; Easterlin 1981). Primary education is the single largest contributor to growth in both the cross-country and cross-regional comparisons and the within-country analyses carried out to explain the East Asian "miracle" of development (box 1.2). Differences in the educational level of the labor force explain about 20 percent of the differences in growth across states in Brazil. They suggest a threshold level of average education somewhere between three and four years of schooling (Lau and others 1993), a result confirmed for Brazil using individual-level information (Griffin and Cox-Edwards 1993) and corroborated for Guatemala (World Bank 1994d).

The East Asian high-growth countries invested heavily in both primary and secondary education in an effort to enhance the quality of labor. This effort was

BOX 1.2 EDUCATION AND ECONOMIC GROWTH IN EAST ASIA

Primary education is the largest single contributor to the economic growth rates of the high-performing Asian economies (World Bank 1993a). Investment in physical capital is second, followed by secondary school enrollments and population growth. These results are based on a 113-nation cross-country regression that estimates the relationship between the rate of real per capita income growth, the share of investment in gross domestic product (GDP), and educational attainment.

The high-performing Asian economies show a significantly higher rate of growth attributable to education than all the other economies. When East Asia and Latin America are compared, 34 percent of the predicted difference in growth rates can be attributed to higher investment levels and 38 percent to higher enrollment rates. Similarly, the major difference between East Asia and Sub-Saharan Africa is due to variations in primary school enrollment rates. Investment in physical capital accounts for only 20 percent of the difference.

complemented on the demand side by a pattern of growth that made productive use of labor and by complementary investment in physical capital. Substantial spending on education increased growth. For example, if in 1960 the Republic of Korea had had the same low school enrollment rate as Pakistan, its GDP per capita by 1985 would have been 40 percent lower than it actually was (World Bank 1993a).

Higher education also contributes to self-sustaining growth through the impact of graduates on the spread of knowledge (Becker 1964). Institutions of higher education have the main responsibility for equipping individuals with the advanced knowledge and skills required for positions of responsibility in government, business, and the professions. These institutions produce new scientific and technical knowledge through research and advanced training and serve as conduits for the transfer, adaptation, and dissemination of knowledge generated elsewhere in the world. Estimated social rates of return of 10 percent or more in many low- and middle-income countries indicate that investments in higher education contribute to increases in labor productivity and to higher long-term growth (World Bank 1994e).

Not all of the external effects of higher education—such as the benefits from basic research and from technology development and transfer—are fully reflected in the earnings used in calculating these rates of return. The returns to higher education, as to basic education, are thus greater than those measured using earnings, and it is very possible that the contribution of higher education to growth may increase with levels of technology and as countries achieve universal primary and secondary education.

The external effect of education is important for economic growth and is suggested both by the possibility of a threshold effect at the primary level and by the likely spread of knowledge facilitated by higher education. The new theories of economic growth, like the older theories, show the complementarity of human and physical capital: a higher stock of human capital enhances the rental value of machines; an increasing stock of physical capital boosts the efficiency of educational investment; and general investment plays a weak role in economic growth when not supported by education (Lucas 1988; Becker 1964). Empirical experience in East Asia demonstrates this complementarity, as well as the importance of sound macroeconomic policies in a broadly competitive economy. The latter finding is reinforced by the experience of the former Soviet Union. There, rapid and sustained physical and human capital investment led at first to rapid growth. However, excessive state intervention in the economy, low capital-labor substitution, the nature of economic planning, and—perhaps most importantly—failure to allow the substantial investments in human capital to flourish and to stimulate qualitative improvements led to a lack of productivity growth and, in the long run, to stagnation (Easterly and Fischer 1994).

Labor Market Linkages

The dramatic recent shifts in labor markets brought about by economic reforms, the integration of the world economy, technological change (especially in information technology), and migration have important consequences for education. International trade and the deregulation of economies and labor markets have not only contributed to growth but have also led to changes in the employment structures of advanced, transition, and developing countries. The rate of accumulation of new knowledge and the pace of technological change raise the possibility of sustained growth and more frequent job changes during individuals' lives. Work tasks are becoming more abstract and more removed from the actual physical processes of production, which require less and less manual involvement.

These developments have two important implications for education systems. First, education must be designed to meet economies' increasing demands for adaptable workers who can readily acquire new skills rather than for workers with a fixed set of technical skills that are used throughout their working lives. This need increases the importance of the basic competencies learned in primary and general secondary schools. Second, education systems—primarily at the higher and postgraduate levels—must support the continued expansion of the stock of knowledge.

Major shifts in labor markets occurred during the 1980s, beginning with a reversal of the trend during the 1970s of declining rewards to higher education in advanced market economies. Overwhelming empirical evidence suggests that the rewards to higher education are now increasing in many advanced countries (see, for example, Davis 1992). This trend set in at a time when earnings inequality was growing at unprecedented rates and the average level of schooling in the labor force was very high. The improvement in the position of the more educated in advanced countries, even though their numbers increased, suggests that the demand for more educated workers has increased over time, causing an increase in the earnings premium associated with more schooling. Although schooling and earnings inequality are related, the earnings premium may increase despite an increase in the average level of schooling (or a decrease in the variance of schooling) if the demand for schooling has also increased.

Recent technological changes have involved both the deskilling of many jobs that previously required some skills and a greater demand for workers to fill more highly skilled positions (Blackburn, Bloom, and Freeman 1990; Blackburn 1990). A decreased demand by employers for manual dexterity, physical strength, and traditional craftsmanship has increased the demand for educated over less educated workers, resulting in relative wage increases favoring more educated workers. Thus, technological change leads to increasing inequality (Bound and Johnson 1992).

More educated workers can deal more effectively with a rapidly changing environment (T. W. Schultz 1975; Mincer 1989; World Bank 1991d). Highly educated workers are more likely than unskilled workers to be found in new technology industries, where they are relatively better paid than in traditional industries; this comparative advantage holds true in high-, middle-, and low-income countries (Bartel and Lichtenberg 1987; Loh 1992; Gill and Riboud 1993).

Schooling raises productivity in the market and in the household by enhancing information acquisition; it improves the ability to learn. But if returns from investments in schooling are to be realized, the scope for productive learning has to be expanded through technical innovation and changes in market and political regimes. The introduction of new technologies can raise the returns to schooling if the new technology increases rather than decreases the need for learning or the scope for misuse of inputs. For example, the "green revolution" in agriculture led to an increased premium for acquisition of information. The new high-yielding imported seed varieties that were the engines of growth of the green revolution were significantly more sensitive to the use of such inputs as water and fertilizer. Farmers formerly engaged in "traditional" farming practices faced the challenge of mastering the appropriate allocation of inputs in order to realize large potential payoffs, and the continuing introduction of new seeds every few years may have raised the returns to skills in information decoding (Rosenzweig 1995).

Relative poverty is generally reduced as the labor force becomes more educated. Evidence for some low- and middle-income countries indicates that equality in schooling corresponds to equality in earnings over the period of the 1980s, in contrast to the situation prevailing in industrial countries (see Patrinos 1994). An increase in the number of educated workers leads to decreased earnings differentials between them and the less educated. This effect is reflected in declining education-earnings premiums as education expands (Psacharopoulos 1989) and in declining wage differentials in the 1970s and 1980s in such countries as Brazil, Colombia, Indonesia, Korea, and Venezuela (Davis 1992; McMahon and Boediono 1992).

Not only is the level of education important in adapting to rapidly changing labor markets; so is its content. It is often suggested, particularly at times of growing youth unemployment, that the school curriculum should be vocationalized or that technical skills should be taught in secondary school in order to equip school leavers for work in the modern sector. Skills training can indeed increase labor market productivity and earnings, but only when the skills are actually used in employment. International experience suggests that vocational and technical education and training are most effective when they follow a sound general education and are job-related. In practice, many countries, especially East Asian countries and members of the OECD, are moving to increase the technology content of general education and the general content of vocational education at the upper-secondary level and to provide many more course options. The effect on employment and earnings of this convergence of the two upper-secondary curricula has yet to be evaluated. Comparative evaluations of earlier, more differentiated, general and vocational secondary curricula indicate clearly, however, that the rate of return to investment has been much higher in general than in vocational secondary education (Psacharopoulos 1987).

The roles of the different educational levels are thus becoming clearer with these labor market changes. Primary and secondary schools focus on basic general competencies—language, science and mathematics, and, increasingly, communications skills, as well as the development of attitudes necessary for the workplace. These competencies provide the foundation for subsequent education and training; even vocational secondary education is becoming more general. Further education and training then consist of the acquisition of academic and vocational skills, in institutions of higher education and in specialized on-the-job training, with periodic updating through work-related continuing education (OECD 1994a).

Poverty Reduction

The low earnings of the poor are partly the result of their relatively lower human capital endowments and partly of labor market discrimination. Education can help with the first, but other steps are necessary to deal with the second. The differential in earnings between women and men in Latin America, for instance, is little explained by differences in human capital (Psacharopoulos and Tzannatos 1992). By contrast, human capital endowments explain most of the overall earnings differential between minority and majority male indigenous workers in Bolivia and between monolingual Guaraní speakers and Spanish speakers in Paraguay. If the relatively poorer Guaraní speakers of Paraguay had the same schooling level as Spanish speakers, the earnings differential would disappear.

Education can therefore make a significant contribution to the reduction of poverty. It confers skills, knowledge, and attitudes that increase the productivity of the poor's labor by increasing their output as farmers and, when discrimination is absent, their access to jobs in both the formal and the informal sectors. Studies have found that a farmer with four years of complete schooling has a much higher productivity than one with no education (Lockheed, Jamison, and Lau 1980; Moock 1994). Education also makes workers in industry more productive (Haddad and others 1990) and can contribute to entrepreneurship (World Bank 1991d).

The creation of human capital is the creation and distribution of new wealth. It contributes to the reduction of both absolute and relative poverty, but it can take a whole generation to have an effect—in contrast to the more rapid effects of redistributing existing capital, through, for example, tax reform and land reform. Resources invested today in education may lead to less poverty only after several years, when the poor whose human capital has been enhanced start to benefit from increased earnings, greater ability in self-employment, and improved efficiency in the use of household resources (T. W. Schultz 1982).

In many developing countries the link between the labor market and the education system that is most important for the poor is the urban informal sector. In Sub-Saharan Africa during the 1980s, for example, about 15 million jobs were created in the informal sector, compared with only 1 million in the urban modern sector. Since the poor often find it difficult to obtain employment in the modern sector, increasing the productivity of workers in the informal sector is an effective way to reduce poverty (Moock, Musgrove, and Stelcner

1990). In these circumstances, as for the modern sector, a sound general education may be more effective, and far more cost-effective, than providing specific vocational and technical skills, as it equips workers to acquire skills on the job.

Studies on the determinants of earnings show that the early home environment plays an important role in the development of a child's intellectual ability. For example, pre-school-age children from lower socioeconomic groups perform substantially worse on tests of cognitive development than do children from higher-income groups (Selowsky 1983). These differences can be attributed to malnutrition, lack of sanitation and health facilities, lack of parental stimulation, and other environmental deficits surrounding children living in poverty. It has also been shown that early childhood interventions (such as the provision of health care, education, and nutrition) can have a positive impact on the lives of children from poor backgrounds (Halpern 1986). Various attempts to equalize the opportunities of children from disadvantaged backgrounds have been made, but they often start too late. Research shows that by age three or four, children have already been conditioned by their family environment (Selowsky 1980; Young 1994). There is a need, therefore, to invest more in early childhood programs designed to enhance the growth and development of children (Myers 1992) and in subsequent programs to sustain the advantages provided by early interventions.

Fertility and Health

The more educated a woman, the lower her fertility (figure 1.1; see also World Bank 1991d, 1993f). Education influences fertility through higher age at marriage for women and increased contraceptive use. For example, age at marriage has been rising steadily in North African countries, largely as a result of school attendance (Westoff 1992). In Honduras, Indonesia, Kenya, and Mexico schooled women desire fewer children, and they express this desire through a higher rate of contraceptive use.

The more educated the parents, particularly the mother, the lower is maternal mortality and the healthier is the child. Parental education is significantly associated with the health status of children (defined by a reduction in mortality or an improvement in chances of survival), even after controlling for socioeconomic status and access to health services (Rodríguez and Cleland 1980; United Nations 1986; Cleland and Wilson 1987; Hobcraft 1993). Rising levels of maternal education reduce the odds of the child's dying before age two (figure 1.2), in both urban and rural settings. On average, child mortality seems to fall by about 8 percent for each additional year of parental schooling, for at least the first eight to ten years of schooling (that is, including secondary as well as primary education).

FIGURE 1.1   TOTAL FERTILITY RATE BY MOTHER'S EDUCATION AND REGION

Total fertility rate

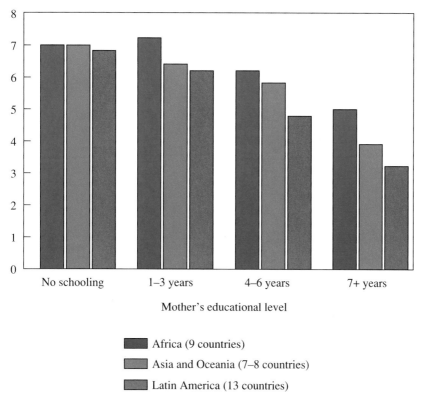

Mother's educational level

Africa (9 countries)
Asia and Oceania (7–8 countries)
Latin America (13 countries)

Note: Data are from demographic surveys taken during the 1970s and 1980s. The total fertility rate represents the number of children that would be born to a woman if she were to live to the end of her childbearing years and bear children at each age in accordance with prevailing age-specific fertility rates.
Source: United Nations 1987.

Parental education influences child mortality through the use of medical services (such as prenatal care and clinic visits) and changes in household health behavior (such as washing hands and boiling water). These behavioral changes may result from perceptual and attitudinal changes and from the ability of the educated (whose incomes are higher than those of the uneducated) to

FIGURE 1.2 CHANCES OF CHILDREN DYING BEFORE AGE TWO BY MOTHER'S EDUCATION

Percentage[a]

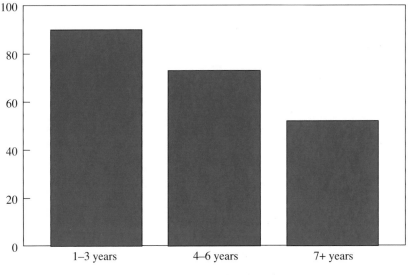

Mother's educational level

Note: Data are from a sample of twenty-five countries in Africa, Asia, and Latin America.
a. Chances of children dying before age two compared with chances for children of mothers with no schooling (represented by 100 percent on vertical axis).
Source: Hobcraft 1993.

afford better nutrition and better health services for their children (Caldwell 1979; Lindenbaum, Chakraborty, and Elias 1989; LeVine and others 1991).

Even before taking account of these effects, the returns to investment in women's education exceed those to men's education for women who obtain employment (Psacharopoulos 1994). When the health and fertility externalities are added, the case for educating girls becomes even stronger. The benefit-cost ratio of these health and fertility externalities in Pakistan, for instance, has been estimated at about 3:1 (table 1.2).

TABLE 1.2. THE EXTERNALITIES OF INVESTING IN GIRLS' EDUCATION, PAKISTAN

Item	Calculation	Cost or benefit (U.S. dollars)
Recurrent cost of one year of education for 1,000 women		30,000
Benefits		
Reduction in child mortality		
Total deaths averted	60	
Set cost (U.S. dollars)	800	
Value of averted deaths		48,000
Reduction in fertility		
Births averted	500	
Set cost (U.S. dollars)	65	
Value of births averted		32,500
Reduction in maternal mortality		
Total maternal deaths averted	3	
Set cost (U.S. dollars)	2,500	
Value of averted maternal deaths		7,500

Source: Summers 1992.

CHAPTER TWO

Achievements and Challenges

THE EDUCATION systems of developing countries have made unprecedented progress in recent years. However, the future holds major challenges for countries at all stages of educational and economic development. Some challenges are of crisis proportions. Enrollments are falling in Africa, and there are still more than a billion illiterate adults in the world. The gender gap between boys' and girls' enrollments is still very wide in the Middle East and in South Asia (where it has not closed at all in the past decade). In low- and middle-income countries the quality of education is poor, compared with OECD countries. Finally, as the pace of technological change quickens, there is a worrying lag between the reform of economic structures and that of education systems, notably in the countries that have embarked on the transition from command to market economies. This chapter identifies these challenges; chapters 3 and 4 describe the ways in which current patterns of education finance and education management are not fully appropriate for meeting them. East Asia's record shows, however, that the challenges can be met if the lessons of successful experience are adopted.

The analysis is mainly regional. Each of the six regions defined by the World Bank for its operational purposes contains a wide range of country conditions, and the findings therefore do not apply to every country in a region. (The regions are described in the Definitions and Data Notes at the front of this book.) The analysis has been severely hampered by the poor availability and quality of data on education and education finance (see the appendix to this chapter). In the graphics, the number of countries included in each region varies depending on data availability. Quantitative conclusions thus represent orders of magnitude and directions of trends rather than precise indications.

Access

The average level of education in developing countries is increasing. For the first time in world history, most children at least start school. By 1990, 76 percent of the 538 million 6-to-11-year-olds in developing countries were in school, up from 48 percent in 1960 and 69 percent in 1980 (UNESCO 1993a). These numbers reflect an increasing ratio of enrollments to the primary-school-age population during the 1980s in every region except Africa. At the secondary level, 46 percent of 12-to-17-year-olds attended school in 1990, the proportion having increased during the 1980s in every region. At the tertiary level, enrollment ratios also increased during the 1980s in every region (figure 2.1).

As a result of these gains, an average 6-year-old in one of the low- and middle-income countries in 1990 could expect to complete 8.5 years of school, up from 7.6 years in 1980; the number of years rose in every region except Africa (figure 2.2). This impressive increase does not, of course, reveal anything about the quality of education.

The achievements in enrollments are all the more remarkable when considered in absolute terms (figure 2.3), as they occurred at a time of general fiscal restraint and, in many regions, of rapid population growth. In Eastern Europe and Central Asia nine or ten years of schooling is the norm. In East Asia and in Latin America and the Caribbean primary education is almost universal. Countries in South Asia and in the Middle East and North Africa are also making steady progress, although those in South Asia still have a considerable distance to go. Sub-Saharan Africa is not doing as well.

With the easing of demographic pressure, coupled with past success in increasing access, especially at the primary level, prospects appear encouraging. The trends outlined here give no reason for complacency, however:

- The absolute number of children in the world who receive no education at all is likely to increase in the next twenty years.

- Only two-thirds of primary school students complete the primary cycle.

- Adult literacy appears likely to remain a major problem, especially for women.

- In part because of past success at the primary level, the demand for secondary and tertiary education is growing faster than many education systems can accommodate.

FIGURE 2.1   GROSS ENROLLMENT RATIOS BY REGION AND LEVEL OF EDUCATION,
1980 AND 1990

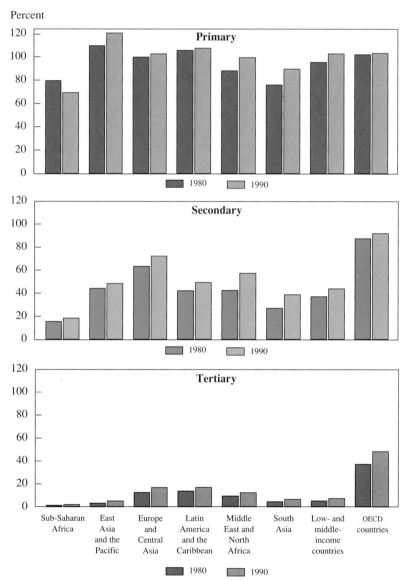

Note: The gross enrollment ratio is the ratio of total enrollment, regardless of age, in a given level of education to the population age group that corresponds to the official school age of this level of education in a given country.

Sources: Based on data in Donors to African Education 1994 and UNESCO 1993a, 1993b.

FIGURE 2.2   EXPECTED YEARS OF SCHOOLING BY REGION, 1980 AND 1990

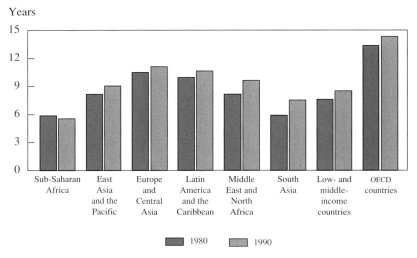

Sources: Based on data in Donors to African Education 1994 and UNESCO 1993a, 1993b.

FIGURE 2.3   PERCENTAGE GROWTH IN ENROLLMENTS BY REGION AND LEVEL
OF EDUCATION, 1980–90

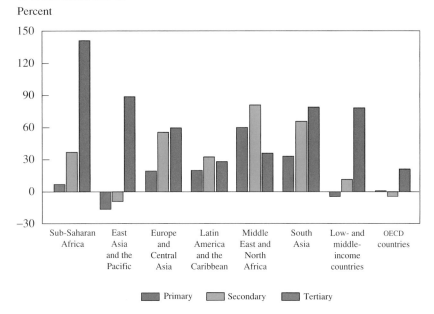

Sources: Based on data in Donors to African Education 1994 and UNESCO 1993a, 1993b.

■ The educational gap between the OECD countries and the transition economies of Eastern Europe and Central Asia is widening.

Demographic Pressure

Demographic pressure on enrollments will remain strong for the next decade
but will start to ease in the next century as the rate of increase falls. The
primary-school-age population in developing countries will increase by about
89 million children between 1990 and 2000 but by only 22 million between
2000 and 2010. Depending on when they started the demographic transition,
some countries now face absolute declines in their school-age populations.
This decline is already occurring in Eastern Europe and Central Asia and will
occur in the first decade of the twenty-first century in East Asia and Latin
America (figure 2.4). Many countries in these regions—for example, Colombia, Indonesia, and Korea—will experience declining school-age populations
even before the region as a whole. This explains the fall in absolute enrollments
at the primary and secondary levels in East Asia, as seen in figure 2.3. An
opposite trend occurred in Africa; there absolute primary enrollments increased,
but not as much as the school-age population, so the gross enrollment ratio fell.
In Africa, South Asia, and the Middle East and North Africa the school-age
population will continue to increase, but more slowly in the first decade of the
2000s than in the 1990s.

The main demographic pressure on enrollments will continue to be in the
three regions with the lowest enrollment ratios for girls and the highest fertility
levels: Africa, South Asia, and the Middle East and North Africa. Between
1990 and 2010 Africa's primary-school-age population is projected to increase
by 59 million, South Asia's by 28 million, and the Middle East and North
Africa region's by 16 million.

The Out-of-School Population

In 1990 about 130 million primary-school-age children—60 percent of them
girls—were not enrolled in school. (The number had been 160 million in 1980.)
The three regions with the greatest demographic pressure account for about two
thirds of all children not enrolled in school. In Africa 50 percent of all primary-
age children are in this category, in South Asia, 27 percent, and in the Middle
East and North Africa, 24 percent. The largest absolute numbers are in South
Asia because of its large population (table 2.1). School-age populations are
growing in all three regions but almost twice as fast in Africa as elsewhere (see
figure 2.4). Enrollment ratios in Africa are low and are decreasing on average;
only 46 percent of primary-age girls are in school. By contrast, primary enroll-

FIGURE 2.4 GROWTH OF THE PRIMARY-SCHOOL-AGE (6–11) POPULATION, 1990–2000 AND 2000–2010

Percent per year

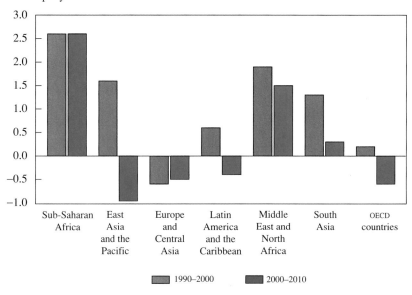

1990–2000   2000–2010

Source: World Bank projections.

ment ratios are increasing for both boys and girls in South Asia and the Middle East, although they are still very low. Unless the pace of enrollment accelerates, the absolute number of children not attending school at all is likely to increase in the next two decades—for the first time since 1960—reaching 145 million in 2000 and 162 million in 2015 (see table 2.1). This outcome would be brought about by continued high population growth rates, combined with falling enrollment ratios in some countries. Despite overall success, at least forty-two low- and middle-income countries have gross primary enrollment ratios below 90 percent (table 2.2). These countries are concentrated in Africa and South Asia, which contain all twelve countries with gross ratios below 50 percent and twenty-one of the thirty countries with ratios between 50 and 90 percent. These two regions also have the highest growth rates of school-age population. Gross enrollment ratios include overage students, but they do indicate trends, if not the absolute change. Net enrollment ratios—the proportion of children of primary

TABLE 2.1   CHILDREN AGE 6–11 OUT OF SCHOOL, 1960–90 AND PROJECTIONS FOR 2000 AND 2015

(millions)

Region	1960		1980		1990		2000		2015	
	Total	Female	Total	Female	Total	Female	Total	Female	Total	Female
All developing countries	165 (52)	96 (62)	158 (31)	94 (38)	129 (24)	77 (29)	145 (22)	85 (27)	162 (23)	92 (27)
Sub Saharan Africa[a]	25 (75)	14 (82)	26 (43)	15 (49)	41 (50)	22 (54)	59 (51)	32 (55)	83 (51)	45 (55)
Middle East[a]	9 (61)	5 (72)	9 (33)	6 (43)	9 (24)	5 (31)	10 (21)	6 (27)	12 (21)	7 (26)
Latin America and the Caribbean	15 (42)	7 (43)	9 (17)	5 (18)	8 (13)	4 (13)	7 (11)	4 (12)	7 (11)	4 (11)
East Asia	67 (47)	39 (56)	55 (25)	32 (30)	26 (14)	14 (16)	27 (13)	15 (14)	21 (12)	11 (12)
South Asia	49 (56)	30 (71)	59 (40)	38 (53)	48 (27)	32 (28)	47 (23)	31 (32)	46 (20)	29 (27)

Note: Numbers in parentheses refer to out-of-school children as a share of all children or of all female children. Regional totals do not add to the total for developing countries, as not all regions are included. These figures are not adjusted for countries where primary education begins at age 7.
a. Four North African countries are included in both Sub-Saharan Africa and Middle East.
Source: UNESCO 1993a.

TABLE 2.2   COUNTRIES WITH PRIMARY GROSS ENROLLMENT RATIO BELOW 90 PERCENT, 1990

Region and country	Gross enrollment ratio	Region and country	Gross enrollment ratio
50–90 percent		Middle East and North Africa	
Sub-Saharan Africa		Dem. Yemen[a]	88
Benin	67	Yemen Arab Rep.[a]	76
Burundi	73	Morocco	65
Central African Rep.	68	Saudi Arabia	77
Chad	64		
Comoros	75	Latin America and the Caribbean	
Côte d'Ivoire	69	Bolivia	85
Gambia, The	64	El Salvador	79
Ghana	77	Guatemala	79
Guinea-Bissau	60	Haiti	56
Malawi	66		
Mauritania	51	*Below 50 percent*	
Mozambique	64	Sub-Saharan Africa	
Nigeria	72	Burkina Faso	37
Rwanda	71	Djibouti	44
Senegal	58	Ethiopia	39
Sudan	50	Guinea	37
Tanzania	69	Liberia	30
Uganda	80	Mali	24
Zaire	76	Niger	29
		Sierra Leone	48
East Asia and Pacific		Somalia	10
Papua New Guinea	72		
		South Asia	
South Asia		Afghanistan	24
Bangladesh	77	Bhutan	25
Nepal	82	Pakistan	42

a. Before unification.
Sources: Donors to African Education 1994; UNESCO 1993b.

school age who are actually enrolled in primary school—would be a better measure of those not in school, but they are not readily available.

Particularly alarming are Africa's falling primary enrollment ratios and, in some countries, falling absolute enrollments. Ratios have not fallen in all African countries. Of the thirty-five countries for which reasonably good data exist, gross primary ratios increased in twenty between 1980 and 1990. In fourteen others, however, including the most populous, the ratios fell, often by a large amount. Thus, the regional average ratio (calculated as the average of country ratios) unweighted by population, fell only from 79 to 78 percent. This may seem minor, but Africa was the only region in the world to register a declining ratio. Because many of the individual countries in which the ratio fell have large populations, the weighted regional average fell from 80 to 69 percent.

Clear evidence is lacking on the reasons for falling enrollments in many African countries. Civil disruption and war explain both declining absolute numbers and declining ratios in several countries, such as Angola and Mozambique. Populations are growing rapidly, despite the high prevalence of HIV/AIDS (box 2.1), and in many countries the supply of education has been unable to keep up with demand, resulting in declining enrollment ratios. A reduction in overage students enrolled does not explain the fall; in six of the seven countries with declining gross ratios for which net ratios are available, the pattern of decline is confirmed. Where absolute enrollments have fallen, however, demand has also fallen due to low quality, poor employment prospects, the need for children's help with household work, and difficulties in paying fees and other school-related expenses (World Bank 1988). Whatever the explanation, even arresting the decline in enrollment ratios will not be

---

BOX 2.1   AIDS AND EDUCATION

Human immunodeficiency virus (HIV), the virus that causes AIDS, is on the increase. The World Health Organization projects that by 2000 as many as 26 million people could carry the virus and that 1.8 million will die of AIDS each year. Most victims are young, in their years of prime working productivity. These deaths could have a profound impact on the demand for education. Children who lose their parents to AIDS are often forced to drop out of school to survive. In Tanzania, for instance, the widespread prevalence of HIV/AIDS is associated with the withdrawal of girls from school and with marriage at an early age, eroding much of the progress made in female education (Ainsworth, Over, and Rwegarulira 1992; Shaeffer 1993).

sufficient to prevent an absolute increase in the number of African children who do not attend school. Simply put, the rate of increase of the school-age population is higher than that of enrollments.

Low Primary Completion Rates

About 30 percent of the children in developing countries who enroll in primary school do not complete it. More than half the countries in East Asia and in the Middle East have completion rates above 80 percent, as do all countries in Europe and Central Asia. By comparison, only one-third of the countries in Latin America and only one-fifth of the countries in Africa and in South Asia have completion rates above 80 percent (UNESCO 1993b). Low completion rates mean that the proportion of children reaching grade 5 is roughly the same in Africa, South Asia, and South America despite very different enrollment ratios in first grade (figure 2.5).

Low primary completion rates result from high repetition and dropout rates. Repetition and dropout are closely linked; the first often leads to the second, although their causes are usually different. On the supply side, the low completion rates may reflect problems with the quality of instruction. On the demand side, families may need children to work (for instance, in agricultural production) and may withdraw children, especially girls, from school temporarily—leading to grade repetition—or even permanently. Dropout clearly affects learning outcomes, but this may not be the case for repetition if students learn more by repeating a grade (Eisemon, Schwille, and Prouty 1992; Psacharopoulos and Velez 1993). Repetition is, of course, costly to the system. And when a student repeats a grade more than once, repetition frequently leads to dropout.

Adult Illiteracy

The combination of an increasing absolute number of children out of school and low primary completion rates means that the formal education system in the poorest countries is likely to continue to be inadequate as a mechanism for overcoming illiteracy. Overall illiteracy rates declined from about 55 percent of all adults in low- and middle-income countries in 1970 to about 35 percent in 1990, but this percentage still represents over 900 million illiterates, up from 840 million in 1970. Many more of the illiterate adults are women than men—a striking aspect of the gender disparities that still characterize many countries. Moreover, although illiteracy rates are declining, they remained at about 50 percent in Africa, the Middle East, and South Asia in 1990 and will not fall much below 40 percent in these regions by 2000 (UNESCO 1990) without new interventions.

FIGURE 2.5   PRIMARY SCHOOL ENROLLMENT AND RETENTION BY REGION, ABOUT 1990

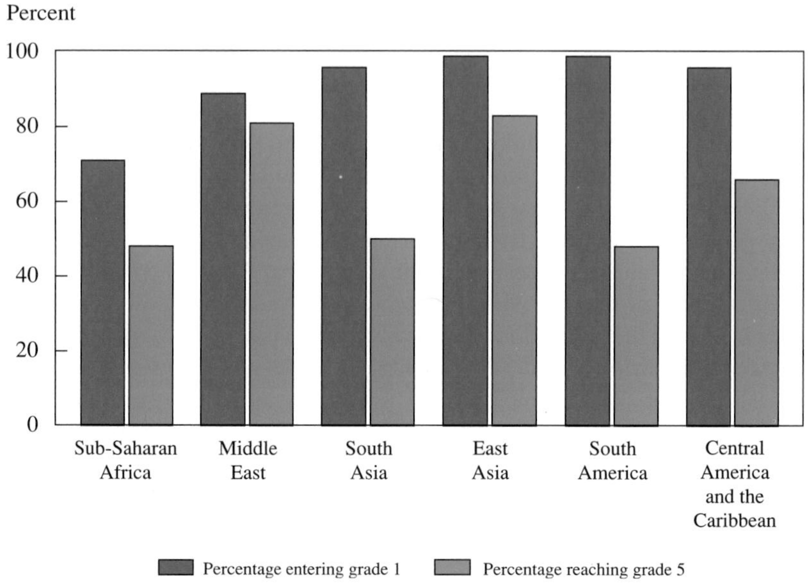

Percent

Percentage entering grade 1   Percentage reaching grade 5

Note: Data do not include overage children and are projected using reconstructed cohort analysis. Regions are those used by UNICEF.
Source: UNICEF 1993.

Growing Unmet Demand for Secondary and Tertiary Education

In most low- and middle-income countries substantially more students seek entrance to secondary and higher-level institutions than there are places available, and the proportion of applicants to successful entrants is increasing. (For detailed evidence on Asia, for instance, see Tan and Mingat 1992.) At the tertiary level this gap partly reflects the provision of free or heavily subsidized public education. At the University of the Punjab in Pakistan, 94 percent of those applying in 1986 were not admitted, up from 91 percent five years before (Butt and Sheikh 1988). In many countries, such as Korea and Thailand, parents often pay for private tutoring outside regular school hours to increase their children's chances of admission. Repetition of the final year of a level—a form of queuing for admission to the next level—is also common. In Mauritius more than 40 percent of secondary students repeat at least one grade to improve their chances of admission to higher education; in Burundi more than 70 percent of primary students repeat the final primary grade.

The growing gap between demand and supply at the secondary level reflects population growth, the increasing proportion of students completing primary school, governments' difficulties in financing an expanded public system, poor parents' difficulties in paying school fees, and restrictions on private schooling. There is strong evidence around the developing world that many 12- to-17-year-olds at the secondary level are not in school because of a lack of places rather than a lack of interest (Holsinger and Baker 1993). In Tanzania, for instance, successful applicants to public secondary schools represented 11 percent of primary school leavers in 1970 but only 1 percent in 1984 because Tanzania neither permitted private secondary schools nor expanded public ones. Since Tanzania started to license private schools in the mid-1980s, enrollments have mushroomed and now exceed those in public secondary schools. This leap demonstrates the previously unmet demand for secondary education. A comparison with Kenya shows clearly that encouraging private schools can help accommodate the demand for secondary education (Knight and Sabot 1990). The same phenomenon is seen in higher education. In Romania secondary school graduates increased more than 20 percent a year during the 1980s. This increase stimulated an enormous pent-up demand for higher education that has led to the appearance of more than sixty private universities since such institutions became legal (World Bank 1991b).

The Widening Gap between OECD Countries and the Transition Economies

A wide gap in years of schooling separates OECD members and the transitional economies of Eastern and Central Europe. Average "expected years in school," defined as the number of years of schooling a child of six can be expected to complete, are considerably lower in the transitional economies than in OECD countries (see figure 2.2). Moreover, this average is a moving target; the expected years an average 6-year-old child in an OECD country will spend in school rose from 13.4 in 1980 to 14.3 in 1990 and will continue to increase in the 1990s. In Eastern and Central Europe expected years in school increased during the 1980s, but initial indications are that the level is falling in the transition economies in the 1990s. As the level of schooling increases in the OECD and falls in the transition economies, the gap is widening.

Equity

Girls, the rural poor, children from linguistic and ethnic minorities, nomads, refugees, street and working children, and children with special needs go to school less than others. In part, this reflects limited access, in part, lower demand. Despite an overall increase in the proportion of girls enrolled in school, boys are still more likely to be enrolled. In 1990 an average 6-year-old girl in a low- or middle-income country could expect to attend school for 7.7 years, up from 6.7 years in 1980; an average 6-year-old boy could expect 9.3 years of education. The gap between boys and girls is widest in South Asia, where in 1990 a girl could expect 6.0 years of schooling and a boy 8.9 years, and in the Middle East, where a girl could expect 8.6 years and a boy 10.7 years. The gender gap is now very small in Eastern and Central Europe and in Latin America, although such regional generalizations mask country exceptions such as Turkey. In all regions except South Asia, the gender gap is closing (figure 2.6).

The gender gap in school enrollments is, of course, not just a matter of access. In addition to a shortage of school spaces for girls, in many countries parents' demand for education for their daughters is low, reflecting both cultural norms and girls' work in and around the home. Literate parents are more likely than illiterate ones to enroll their daughters in school, and the regions with the highest proportions of illiterate adults are therefore those with the widest gender gaps. Overcoming the gender gap will require not only providing

FIGURE 2.6   GENDER GAPS IN EXPECTED YEARS OF SCHOOLING BY REGION, 1980 AND 1990

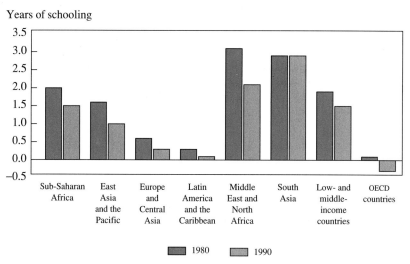

Sources: Based on data in Donors to African Education 1994 and UNESCO 1993a, 1993b.

school places for girls but also overcoming many parents' ignorance of the gains that will result from enrolling their female children.

Rural populations are less educated than urban populations. Only 3 percent of Indonesia's urban population in 1980 had received no schooling, as against 10 percent for the rural population. In Venezuela in 1991, 95 percent of urban 10-to-14-year olds, but only 86 percent of rural children of the same age, were enrolled (World Bank 1993e). Gender differences are particularly acute when disaggregated by urban-rural residence. In Pakistan in 1991 the proportion of girls and boys aged 7 to 14 years who ever attended school was 73 and 83 percent in urban areas, but 40 and 74 percent in rural areas (Sathar and Lloyd 1993). In Egypt 35 percent of rural people are literate, compared with 61 percent of the urban population (World Bank 1991d). Approximately 60 percent of urban students in Colombia complete primary education, but only 20 percent in rural areas do (World Bank 1990b).

Relatively lower enrollments among the poor are most pronounced in higher education, largely as a consequence of inequities at the primary and secondary levels. For example, in the late 1980s, 63 percent of higher-education students in Chile came from the top income quartile of households, and 92 percent of students in Indonesia and 77 percent in Venezuela came from the top income quintile (Tilak 1989; World Bank 1993c, 1993e).

Linguistic minorities also suffer from relatively lower enrollments because they are often poor and because of language policies. Most countries are multilingual, either officially or in practice. More than 5,000 languages and dialects are spoken around the world, including more than 200 in Mexico and more than 400 in India and in Nigeria. Linguistic diversity reflects ethnic diversity and is often associated with high levels of illiteracy. In Guatemala, for instance, 80 percent of the rural indigenous population is illiterate, and indigenous males in the labor force average only 1.8 years of schooling. In rural Peru, where the majority of the population is indigenous, 70 percent of Quechua-speaking people over the age of five have never been to school, compared with only 40 percent of nonindigenous Peruvians (Psacharopoulos and Patrinos 1994).

Others who have difficulty going to school are nomads, refugees, street and working children, and children with learning and physical impairments. Refugees suffer from the unwillingness of host governments to fund expenses for temporary immigrants. Street children suffer from lack of parental guidance, and working children because of the need to contribute to family income. Disease and malnutrition in developing countries result in a high proportion of children with learning and physical impairments, estimated at 10 to 12 percent of all those under age 15. Most of these children with impairments come from poor families, and most lack access to schooling. Official estimates from developing countries suggest that of every hundred children with special needs, only one receives any form of schooling (Mittler, Brouillette, and Harris 1993).

Quality

Quality in education is difficult to define and measure. An adequate definition must include student outcomes. Most educators would also include in the definition the nature of the educational experiences that help produce those outcomes—the learning environment (see Ross and Mählck 1990). On both counts, the quality of education at all levels in low- and middle-income countries is not of the same standard as in OECD countries, although the lack of time-series data on outcomes makes it impossible to discern trends. Furthermore, students in low- and middle-income countries drop out and repeat more than those in high-income countries.

An important indicator of the quality of education is the value added of schooling—a measure of outcomes (Bridge, Judd, and Moock 1979; Lockheed and Hanushek 1988). The value added consists of learning gain and the increased probability of income-earning activity. (The value added of higher education also includes research productivity). Cognitive learning gain can be measured by achievement tests. Measurement of changes in the probability of income-earning activity is extremely difficult, since it is affected by changes in the demand for labor in an economy. For example, a university graduate could receive a quality education in ancient languages, but there might be no demand for such skills.

Recent international comparisons of achievement have been made of 9-year-old and 14-year-old students in reading and in mathematics and science. Although most of the countries included in the comparisons are OECD members, enough developing countries were included to show that test scores in developing countries are lower—in some cases by more than one standard deviation—than the international mean for all countries compared. The reading results for 14-year-olds in Botswana, the Philippines, Thailand, Trinidad and Tobago, Venezuela, and Zimbabwe shown in figure 2.7 illustrate this finding. In Burkina Faso and other Sahelian countries, mean achievement scores sometimes approach randomness, suggesting that students are learning very little (Jarousse and Mingat 1993).

As striking as the lower mean score in developing countries is the greater variation around the mean, both of student scores and of school scores. Some Venezuelan students, for instance, test as high on reading as the international mean; others test in the bottom decile. In the Philippines 15 percent of schools scored higher than the median for all countries in a test of achievement in general science (Lockheed, Fonacier, and Bianchi 1989). The variance in reading achievement in developing countries appears to be related to differences between urban and rural schools, which are many times more pronounced than

FIGURE 2.7 VARIATION IN READING ACHIEVEMENT FOR 14-YEAR-OLDS IN SELECTED COUNTRIES, 1990–91

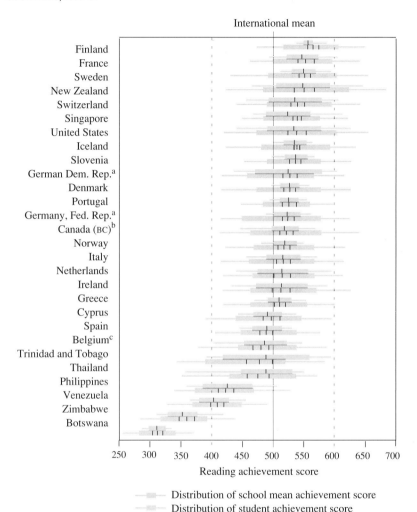

Reading achievement score

Distribution of school mean achievement score
Distribution of student achievement score

Note: For each country, the vertical center line in each bar indicates the mean; the lines parallel to the center line represent +1.96 and –1.96 standard errors of sampling; the end points of the bar indicate the 25th and 75th percentile points; and the ends of the horizontal lines extending from the bar plot the 10th and 90th percentile points. The dotted vertical lines indicate +1 and –1 standard deviation from the mean international student achievement score.
a. Before unification.
b. British Columbia.
c. French-speaking area.
Source: IEA 1994.

FIGURE 2.8   DIFFERENCE IN READING ACHIEVEMENT BETWEEN URBAN AND RURAL
SCHOOLS FOR 14-YEAR-OLDS IN SELECTED COUNTRIES, 1990–91

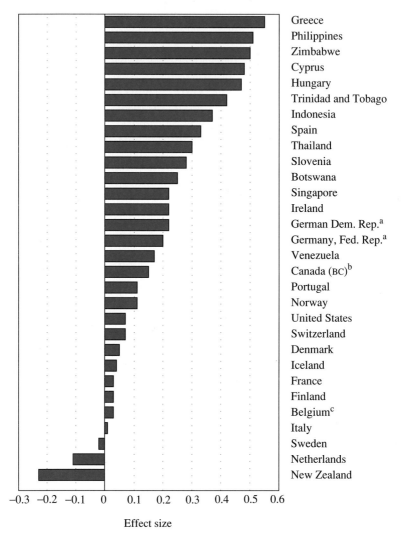

Effect size

Note: The effect size measures the difference between the mean scores for students in urban and rural areas in relation to the pooled standard deviation. An index value less than 0.2 can be considered insignificant, a difference between 0.2 and 0.5, small, and a difference greater than 0.5, moderate to large.
a. Before unification.
b. British Columbia.
c. French-speaking area.
Source: IEA 1994.

in advanced countries (figure 2.8). Raising quality will thus imply not only increasing average performance but also reducing variation across students and schools by making the greatest improvements in the learning environments and performance at the worst schools.

Delays in Reforming Education

A more general and very disturbing issue is the lag between reform of countries' economic systems and that of their education systems. As chapter 1 showed, technological progress is accelerating, and along with it the pace of change of economic structures. In these circumstances, delays in reforming the education system to keep pace with the economic system can imply lower growth and more poverty than would otherwise occur. This dynamic is particularly pronounced in the former socialist economies of Eastern and Central Europe, where many of the impressive educational legacies of the communist period are now threatened by austerity, uncertainty, and too slow a response by the education system to political and economic changes (box 2.2).

The education systems that Eastern and Central Europe inherited from the socialist period were designed for a centrally planned economy that required labor with specialized professional, technical, and vocational skills. The result was a proliferation of narrow training programs. Because resource allocations were determined by politically established plan objectives, there was little need for well-trained managers, for a skilled labor force, or for citizens capable of showing individual initiative. Studies in the applied social sciences and humanities were discouraged. Teaching and learning practices allowed relatively little scope for independent studies or for development of critical thinking skills.

Nevertheless, the educational legacies of socialism are impressive. They include almost universal adult literacy; universal access to primary and lower-secondary education; high average levels of educational attainment; significant reduction of unequal access associated with gender, ethnicity, rural residence, and socioeconomic status; the provision of high-quality compulsory education; the establishment of a large network of preschools; and international excellence in many fields of advanced scientific training and research. These accomplishments are now threatened by austerity, by political and economic uncertainty, and especially by the slow response of education systems throughout the region to the emergence of participatory political systems and market economies and the consequent demand for new kinds of skills.

The failure to adjust education systems is just as serious, if not as visible, in countries in other regions in the face of increasing global economic competition and more open markets. These changes underline the need for a labor force with ever higher average levels of skills and knowledge and for more even

BOX 2.2   EDUCATION IN EASTERN AND CENTRAL EUROPE DURING THE POLITICAL AND ECONOMIC TRANSITION

Despite the paucity of reliable time-series data, there is evidence of decline in important educational indicators in the transition economies during the 1990s. In Russia, for example, enrollment in higher education contracted by 5 percent and enrollment in technical and vocational institutions by 9 and 7 percent, respectively. Preschool enrollments dropped by 22 percent between 1991 and 1993. Between 1992 and 1993 alone, total educational expenditures fell 29 percent in real terms. In a country where state control produced a high degree of uniformity in educational financing, variations in educational expenditures by rich and poor localities are increasing.

In Poland, as in Russia, educational expenditures have declined as a proportion of a shrinking GDP, even though Poland's economy is now growing. In Bulgaria, Hungary, Romania, and several other Eastern and Central European countries, education budgets have been better protected, but public expenditures have declined in real terms. In Romania per student expenditures in public higher education decreased 36 percent between fiscal 1990 and 1993, although enrollments increased by about 44 percent.

A vibrant private education sector has developed in Bulgaria, Estonia, Romania, Russia, and elsewhere as an alternative to state-provided compulsory and higher education. The curricula of many of these institutions emphasize foreign language training, management, and other market-

distribution of these skills within the population. The East Asian countries, which have generally invested heavily in basic human capital for both men and women, are outstanding examples of what can be achieved when the education system is reformed along with the economic system.

Appendix. The Poverty of Education Data

Data and research on education are generally insufficient for monitoring, policymaking, and resource allocation. In Syria, for instance, 50 percent more students recently completed secondary school than had been estimated, with enormous repercussions for the higher education system. Estimates by Uganda's Ministry of Finance showed 85,000 primary-level teachers in the system in 1992, while the Ministry of Education counted 140,000 (Puryear 1995). In Mauritius the rationality of the reform of basic education in the 1990s was undermined by the poor quality and analysis of data on education (Bhowon and Chinapah 1993).

oriented skills. Nevertheless, legislation to accredit private institutions and recognize the qualifications they award has been introduced only recently in a few countries, such as Romania, which by 1994 had sixty-six private universities.

Reform efforts during the first years of transition focused on depoliticizing school curricula and management, reestablishing the political autonomy of universities, redefining the educational rights of ethnic and linguistic minorities, and, especially in Russia, increasing local control of schooling. Guarantees of employment for graduates of the education system were abrogated, as were policies that mandated state-owned enterprises to provide and finance various education and training activities. The principle of cost-sharing in noncompulsory education was embraced, either formally through legislation or informally by the introduction of new fees.

In most countries in Eastern and Central Europe, however, structures for administering and allocating public funding for education have remained largely unchanged, notwithstanding a plethora of reform proposals. One consequence of the lack of comprehensive reform is the increasing reliance on decrees and regulations for managing education systems. In Romania, which has not as yet passed an organic law on education, the government has found it necessary to issue more than 2,000 temporary decrees and regulations since 1990 to manage the higher education subsector (Eisemon and others forthcoming; Laporte and Schweitzer 1994; Vlasceanu 1993; World Bank 1994k, 1994l).

The problems arise mainly because:

■ Existing education statistics are generally not reliable.

■ Statistics are often out of date and hence of limited use in informing policy decisions.

■ Statistics are often collected as a matter of course, with too little critical reflection on the underlying theoretical framework, the comparative perspective, and the purposes for which the data are intended.

■ The information collected focuses more on counting inputs than on assessing achievement and monitoring labor market outcomes.

■ Educational research is usually not available or is not used to complement statistics in monitoring education systems.

Efforts to improve the situation are under way in many countries. The OECD initiative to develop a limited set of comparable indicators of national education systems is a large cooperative project designed to improve the reliability, timeliness, policy relevance, and comparability of a core set of essential statistics on education finance, expenditure, and student achievement (OECD 1993; Tuijnman and Bottani 1994). Similar initiatives are being launched elsewhere, particularly in Asia. And some countries in Latin America have reasonably good data.

Although laudable, these efforts do not go far enough because they do not address the principal causes of the problem in a global perspective. In most countries there is little incentive, and often little funding, for the collection and analysis of data, especially that needed for the assessment of learning, and the monitoring and evaluation of educational developments. In many countries fear of the potential political repercussions of reporting negative trends and weaknesses in the education system is an impediment. Internationally, global leadership is lacking. UNESCO, for instance, compiles international statistics supplied by its member countries but does not verify them. A major international cooperative effort, spearheaded by UNESCO and the World Bank, to improve education data and research in developing countries is now beginning. This work is perhaps similar to the efforts in the 1950s that led to international consensus on the value of using the United Nations system of national economic accounts—a practice that continues to the present.

CHAPTER THREE

Public Finance for Efficiency and Equity

Public finance is the main instrument for implementing public priorities, and there is a strong rationale for public intervention in the financing of education. In general, public investment accounts for about two-thirds of all education spending, although the share varies from as much as 93 percent in Hungary to below 50 percent in Uganda (table 3.1). Public spending on education is often inefficient, however, when it is misallocated across levels and within levels, and it is inequitable when qualified potential students are unable to enroll in institutions because there are no educational opportunities available or because they are unable to pay or to obtain financing.

The Rationale for Public Finance

The high private rates of return to investments at all levels of education justify large investments by individuals. They also justify self-financing by families or students, through immediate or deferred cost-sharing. Despite these high private returns and the justification for private finance, there is also a strong case for public intervention, especially for basic education, for reasons of income distribution, capital market imperfections, information asymmetries, and externalities. In fact most governments are heavily involved in all levels of education—an activity which in many cases takes up a significant portion of public expenditures.

TABLE 3.1   EDUCATION EXPENDITURE BY SOURCE OF FUNDS, ALL LEVELS OF EDUCATION COMBINED, SELECTED COUNTRIES, 1991
(percent)

Group and country	Public sources	Private sources
OECD countries		
Australia	85.0	15.0
Canada	90.1	9.9
Denmark	99.4	0.6
Finland	92.3	7.7
France	89.7	10.3
Germany	72.9	27.1
Ireland	93.4	6.6
Japan	73.9	26.1
Netherlands	98.0	2.0
Spain	80.1	19.9
United States	78.6	21.4
Low- and middle-income countries		
Haiti	20.0	80.0
Hungary	93.1	6.9
India	89.0	11.0
Indonesia[a]	62.8	37.2
Kenya[b] (1992/93)	62.2	37.8
Uganda (1989/90)	43.0	57.0
Venezuela (1987)	73.0	27.0

a. Public institutions only. Private sources refer to households only.
b. Primary and secondary levels only. Private sources refer to households only.
Sources: Noss 1991; OECD 1993; Tilak 1993; World Bank 1993c, 1993e, 1994g, 1994m.

Income Distribution

Education can reduce income inequality by promoting productivity gains in agriculture and facilitating the absorption of labor into the modern industrial sector. Equality of distribution of education usually results in equality of distribution of income. Education opens new opportunities for the poor and so increases social mobility. Public spending on basic education definitely helps the poor, for two reasons. First, because the poor tend to have large families, a larger subsidy accrues to a poor family than to a rich one. Second, the rich may opt out and buy private education, again increasing the amount of the subsidy that flows to the poor.

Not all groups in society can afford the direct and indirect costs associated with investing in education, and so the state has a role in promoting equality of opportunity. If education were provided under market conditions, only those who could afford to pay tuition fees could enroll. Not only would there be underinvestment from the social point of view, but income inequalities would be preserved from one generation to the next, since education is itself a determinant of lifetime income.

Capital Market Imperfections

The private purchase of schooling, especially of higher education, is beyond the means of many poor families. Most credit markets do not provide an effective solution because of strong imperfections that reduce participation, particularly by very poor people. In principle, the budget constraints can be overcome by borrowing, given the high private rates of return to education. However, there are high risks for both borrowers and lenders in educational financing, and banks do not accept the promise of future earnings as collateral. The failure of the capital market thus affects not only lower-income groups but also middle-income groups that cannot finance tertiary education without credit.

Information Asymmetries

Parents with little education tend to be less informed than better-educated parents about the benefits or quality of education. In the United Kingdom working-class parents tend not to encourage their children to aspire to an university education (Barr 1993).The capital market for education is far from perfect. Students from poor households are understandably reluctant to saddle themselves with debt or to enter into fixed obligations because they do not know their future incomes. Furthermore, those from poor backgrounds tend to underestimate their prospects. Lenders hesitate to accept risks backed only by the uncertain future incomes of reluctant debtors (Arrow 1993).

Externalities

The benefits of education accrue not only to its direct recipients but also to society at large. In the absence of government provision, expenditures on education are smaller than would be desirable. According to an adaptation of new growth theory, a worker's productivity is affected by the average level of human capital, as well as by the worker's own human capital (Lucas 1988). Widespread public education at the basic level may be a threshold for development. The optimal distribution of education for maximizing the spillover effects associated with human capital and taking advantage of these potential threshold levels would appear to be a distribution that is equitable. External effects on health and fertility are not maximized on the basis of private spending alone but can be captured for society as a whole through public spending.

Misallocation among Education Subsectors

In low- and middle-income countries the rates of return to investments in basic (primary and lower-secondary) education are generally greater than those to higher education. Therefore basic education should usually be the priority for public spending on education in those countries that have yet to achieve near-universal enrollment in basic education. Indeed, in most countries the highest share of public spending on education goes to primary education (table 3.2). In all regions except South Asia, moreover, the share of public education spending going to secondary education increased during the 1980s (figure 3.1), reflecting growing enrollments and the near achievement of universal primary education in several regions. Few low- and middle-income countries, except those of Europe and Central Asia and some countries in East Asia and the Middle East, have achieved near-universal secondary education. Hence the increasing share of public spending going to higher education during the 1980s in regions without high primary and secondary enrollment ratios is unlikely to be efficient, as the rates of return to primary and secondary education are likely to be higher in most countries. Similarly, the declining share of public spending going to higher education in the Europe and Central Asia region may

TABLE 3.2   PUBLIC RECURRENT EXPENDITURE ON EDUCATION BY LEVEL, 1990
(percent)

Region	Primary	Secondary	Tertiary
Low- and middle-income countries			
Sub-Saharan Africa (22)	42.9	28.0	19.7
East Asia and the Pacific (4)	41.3	30.5	14.8
Europe and Central Asia (5)	49.3	26.8	15.9
Latin America and the Caribbean (11)	39.4	28.5	18.4
Middle East and North Africa (3)	36.0	41.5	16.1
South Asia (3)	41.5	30.4	13.9
OECD countries (15)	30.7	39.0	20.6

Note: Unweighted averages; figures in parentheses refer to the number of countries in the regional sample.
Sources: Donors to African Education 1994; UNESCO database.

FIGURE 3.1   CHANGE IN ALLOCATION OF PUBLIC RECURRENT EXPENDITURE
ON EDUCATION BY REGION AND LEVEL, 1980–90

Percent

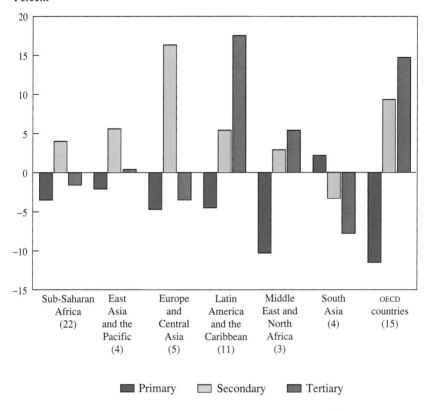

■ Primary   □ Secondary   ■ Tertiary

Note: Percentages are unweighted averages. Figures in parentheses refer to the number of countries in the
regional sample.
Sources: Donors to African Education 1994; UNESCO database.

be inappropriate, depending on the returns to investment at different levels of
education.

Even though spending per higher education student fell as a proportion of
spending per primary student in all regions (table 3.3), subsidization of higher
education is still very high. This subsidization increases the demand for higher
education, even though education at that level is generally less efficient for
society as a whole in countries that have yet to achieve universal primary and

TABLE 3.3   PUBLIC SPENDING PER STUDENT: HIGHER EDUCATION AS A MULTIPLE
OF PRIMARY EDUCATION, 1980–90

Region	1980	1990
Low- and middle-income countries		
Sub-Saharan Africa (8)	65.3	44.1
East Asia and the Pacific & South Asia (4)	30.8	14.1
Latin America and the Caribbean (4)	8.0	7.4
Middle East and North Africa (2)	14.6	8.2
OECD countries (15)	3.0	2.5

Note: Unweighted averages; figures in parentheses refer to the number of countries in the regional sample.
Source: UNESCO database.

secondary education. The subsidization of higher education is most acute in
Africa. Although private rates of return to higher education are 2.5 times higher
than social rates (see table 1.1), public spending per student in higher education
in Africa is about 44 times spending per student in primary school. The share of
tertiary education in public spending on education is higher in Africa than in
any other region, at the same level as in OECD countries, according to the
UNESCO database.

Misallocation within Education Subsectors

Inefficiencies, which are prevalent within all education subsectors, reflect an
inefficient mix of inputs, such as staff and instructional materials. They can also
result from high repetition and dropout rates. For effective learning, the input
mix inevitably varies from country to country and institution to institution,
according to local conditions. Important broad guidance about the internal
efficiency of education systems can come, however, from international comparisons and interschool comparisons, especially with regard to student-teacher
ratios and school buildings.

The student-teacher ratio is one overall measure of staff efficiency, although it excludes nonteaching staff and shows systemwide averages, not actual class size. To take one example, China's student-teacher ratio is 25:1 at the
primary level and 17:1 at the secondary level, compared with an average in
Asia of 34:1 and 23:1. Chinese teachers teach for only 12–18 hours a week,
compared with 20–25 hours a week in other countries (Tsang 1993). Schools in
low- and middle-income countries could save costs and improve learning by

increasing student-teacher ratios. They would thereby use fewer teachers and would be able to allocate resources from teachers to other inputs that improve achievement, such as textbooks and in-service teacher training, as discussed in chapter 4. (In practice, such savings are rarely allocated to other inputs.) Yet in all regions except South Asia primary and secondary student-teacher ratios are decreasing (figure 3.2). In Africa the number of teachers increased by 24 percent between 1985 and 1990, while the enrollment ratio declined by 3 percent (Donors to African Education 1994).

The scope for improving efficiency through modest increases in student-teacher ratios is enormous because teacher costs typically account for about two-thirds of total spending on education (UNESCO 1993b). In Botswana a gain of one year of learning per grade could be achieved in junior secondary school by reducing class size (requiring more teachers) at a cost of $9,414 per grade, or by introducing supplementary reading materials at a cost of $727, or by increasing in-service teacher training, at a cost of $328 (Fuller, Hua, and Snyder 1994). Some countries, such as Bangladesh, Malawi, and Namibia, where the first two grades often have more than sixty students per teacher, would benefit greatly from significantly reducing rather than increasing class size.

School buildings are not entirely necessary for obtaining desired academic outcomes. Indeed, the first "academe" in Europe was a public grove of trees where Plato taught. Even today, learning occurs despite the absence of buildings in many countries, including parts of rural India. However, school buildings are everywhere acknowledged as conventional locations for teaching and learning. There are many opportunities for increasing efficiency in constructing and using buildings, thus saving resources for other purposes. Many countries, particularly those in Africa with colonial legacies, adopt expensive design standards and use imported construction materials. This is evident in comparative construction costs for World Bank postsecondary education projects in Africa and Asia in the early 1980s: the estimated total construction cost per boarding place in nonuniversity education in West Africa was nearly double that in South Asia and 50 percent higher than that in East Asia and the Pacific (Singh 1990). In some African countries the annualized capital costs of new school facilities are as much as 80 percent of annual recurrent costs (World Bank 1988).

Construction costs can be cut by simplifying designs and by using appropriate materials and community labor, supervised by trained engineers to maintain safety standards (for example, earthquake-proof construction for certain regions). Cost-sharing with communities in school construction is common, especially at the primary level. These approaches have brought down costs in World Bank projects in India, Mexico, and Senegal by as much as 50 percent. Flexible floor plans can also improve space utilization by accommodating changes in enroll-

FIGURE 3.2   PRIMARY AND SECONDARY STUDENT-TEACHER RATIOS, 1980 AND 1990

Number of students per teacher[a]

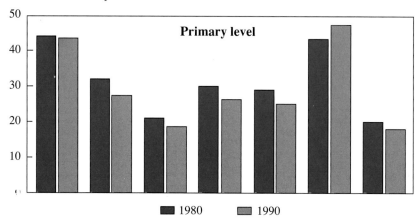

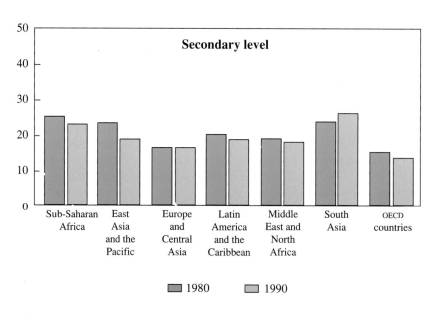

a. Unweighted averages.
Source: Based on data in UNESCO 1993b.

ments. For example, multipurpose school buildings in Bangladesh have removable partitions to permit different class sizes and accommodate large school and community gatherings. There are, however, tradeoffs between flexibility and instructional effectiveness.

It is also critical to maintain a building's physical plant and equipment, yet frequently sufficient funds are not allocated. This oversight has been a particular problem in Africa, where responsibility for school maintenance often rests with the central government rather than the local level (World Bank 1988).

More intensive use of existing school buildings can reduce the need for new school construction. In Jordan a systematic program of school consolidation has led to the closing of about 1,000 schools. In Thailand lower-secondary classes now share with primary classes buildings that were previously used only as primary schools. Another way schools can be used more intensively is to adopt multiple shifts, which reduce per student capital costs. For example, the per student costs of school construction and furnishing in Jamaica are J$1,500 for single-shift schools, J$1,139 for overlapping double shifts, and J$1,027 for end-on double shifts, in which the second shift starts after the first-shift pupils leave (Bray 1990; Leo-Rhynie 1981). Project preparation estimates in Zambia show that maximum use of multiple shifts in primary grades 1 through 7 can reduce per student construction costs by half (Bray 1990; Kelly and others 1986).

Multiple shifts can reduce achievement, however, if they lead to reduced instruction time per student. Multiple-shift schools therefore often increase the number of days of school attendance per year to compensate for a shorter number of hours per day. Such techniques have been used extensively and successfully in Korea, Malaysia, and other East Asian countries. If annual instructional hours are maintained, there is no significant loss in quality compared with single-shift schools (Bray 1990; Leo-Rhynie 1981).

Multigrade teaching, in which one teacher instructs more than one grade, can be cost-effective in rural areas, where teachers are often scarce and classes are often small because few children are in a particular grade. A successful example is the Escuela Nueva program in Colombia (Thomas and Shaw 1992). Multigrade teaching can reduce the costs of repetition and dropout if it enables students to repeat only the parts of the curriculum they found difficult. The overall costs of multigrade teaching are higher than for single-grade schemes, however, because of the need for special teacher training, study guides, and teaching materials. In Colombia these needs raise unit costs by 5 to 10 percent compared with costs for single-grade teaching, largely because teacher training is three times as costly. Since learning achievement in language and mathematics is higher, however, the extra costs are justified by the benefit-cost calculation (Psacharopoulos, Rojas, and Velez 1993). In Colombia and other Latin American countries multigrade schools tend to perform better than single-grade schools (Velez, Schiefelbein, and Valenzuela 1993). Multigrade teaching is not successful where single-grade techniques are simply applied without adaptation to a multigrade class, as in Pakistan.

At the higher level, buildings can sometimes be dispensed with altogether. Open universities for motivated higher education students, for instance, are much less costly than conventional universities. In Korea the unit costs for distance learning are only 10 percent those of residential students. Similar results were found in Thailand (14 percent), Pakistan (22 percent), and China (50 percent) (Lockheed, Middleton, and Nettleton 1991). The lower costs result from the much higher student-staff ratios. Dropout rates are very high in distance higher education courses—typically 50 percent or more—and so costs per graduate are double the costs per student. In China, where dropout rates in distance higher education are 69 percent, the unit cost per graduate is higher than in a conventional university. A proper comparison of distance and conventional higher education would involve calculating the returns to each. This comparison has not generally been made, largely because of the unavailability of data on graduate earnings according to type of higher education institution. It has, however, been calculated for Thailand, where the cost per student at open universities is only one-fiftieth that at conventional ones but the earnings of open university graduates are only 2 percent less, on average, than those of private university graduates (Tan 1991).

Repetition and dropout are a further result of inefficiency, although their causes are complex and some repetition can even improve achievement. They are most pronounced in Africa and Latin America but are declining in both regions. The simple solution to repetition is automatic promotion. However, this solution is frequently not possible, when repetition is a form of queuing for entry to the next level of schooling, or not desirable, when repetition occurs because students have failed to master certain skills. Improving access and quality are, in general, more appropriate solutions to the problems of repetition and dropout.

Inequitable Public Spending

Although public spending on primary education generally benefits the poor, total public spending on education in low- and middle-income countries often favors the affluent, largely because relatively fewer poor children attend secondary and higher education institutions. In developing countries as a whole, 71 percent of school-age children share only 22 percent of overall public resources for education, whereas the 6 percent who receive higher education get 39 percent of public resources (Mingat and Tan 1985).

Various criteria can be used to assess the equity impact of public spending. A weak technical criterion is whether the poor receive a share of the public financing subsidy larger than their share in national income. If so, the distribution of the subsidy improves the distribution of real income, and the relative size of the per capita subsidy expressed as a proportion of per capita income is larger for the poor than for the better-off. A stronger technical criterion is whether the poor receive a share of the subsidy that is larger than their share in the population, meaning that the absolute size of the per capita subsidy is larger for the poor. An even stronger, and better, criterion is whether public expenditure, including loan guarantees, is arranged so that no qualified student is unable to enroll in education at any level because of inability to pay. There is no simple measure of this criterion, which hinges on the existence of an appropriate selection mechanism at the postcompulsory level that can be used to define "qualified." In the absence of such a mechanism, the weaker technical measure can be used as a minimal criterion.

In Indonesia in 1989, Kenya in 1992, and Colombia in 1974, Lorenz curves for the distribution of the education subsidy compared with the distribution of personal income show similar patterns (figure 3.3). The total education subsidy is more evenly distributed than personal income; its Lorenz curve lies above the income distribution curve. Overall, the education subsidy only weakly favors the poor, however, because it lies below the 45° diagonal indicating equal shares of the total subsidy. The only line above the diagonal in all three cases is the curve for primary education, which shows a strong pro-poor distribution: lower-income individuals receive a larger share of the primary school subsidy than their share in the overall population. The secondary and tertiary education subsidies do not even remotely favor the poor because so few poor children are enrolled at these levels. Not only does public spending on secondary and tertiary education favor the better-off in absolute terms (their Lorenz curves lie below the 45° diagonal); it is less equal than even the distribution of personal income. Rich households receive a larger share of postprimary education subsidies than their share of total income. Given these results for the relatively weak technical criteria, it is clear that education spending by the public sector is very inequitable in terms of the more intuitive criterion that no qualified person should be unable to enroll in education because of inability to pay.

It is possible to reallocate total public expenditure by encouraging the enrollment of the poor so that spending is no longer biased in favor of the affluent. During the 1970s and 1980s Colombia increased poor family enrollments and improved the targeting of its spending on secondary and tertiary

FIGURE 3.3   DISTRIBUTION OF SUBSIDIES FOR EDUCATION IN COLOMBIA, INDONESIA, AND KENYA, SELECTED YEARS

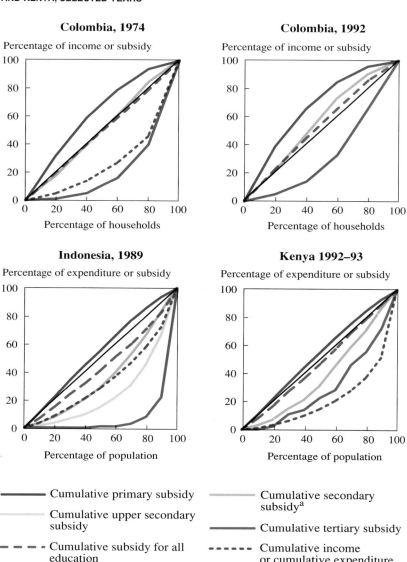

a. For Indonesia, lower secondary. Upper secondary subsidy is shown for Indonesia only.
Sources: For Colombia, 1974, Selowsky 1979; for Colombia, 1992, World Bank 1994a; for Indonesia, World Bank 1993c; for Kenya, World Bank 1994f.

education. As a result, education spending as a whole in 1992 benefited the poor, even though spending on tertiary education continued to favor the upper socioeconomic classes (see figure 3.3).

Public expenditure is also biased against the rural population. This pattern is consistent with the bias against the poor, as the incidence of poverty is usually greater in rural than in urban areas. In Indonesia in 1989, for instance, the monthly subsidy for all education programs averaged Rp.1,520, but the average for the urban population was Rp.1,894, compared with Rp.1,366 for the rural population (World Bank 1993c). In China primary education in the rural areas that contain 70 percent of the population is financed mainly by parents and communities through cash and in-kind contributions to teachers' salaries and school construction. Urban primary and secondary schools are financed by provincial, town, and district governments. Chinese universities charged no tuition before 1989 (Tsang 1993).

Spending on higher education also illustrates the bias against the poor. Spending more public funds per higher education student than per primary student is inefficient in most countries because the social returns are generally lower to higher education than to primary education, at least in countries with less than universal primary and secondary enrollments. It is also inequitable: those students who gain access to higher education receive a larger absolute subsidy than those at lower levels, and higher education students come disproportionately from richer families (table 3.4), which are better able to pay for higher studies. Yet public higher education is free, or almost free, to students in most countries. In only twenty developing countries do tuition fees account for more than 10 percent of recurrent expenditures. There are important regional

TABLE 3.4   HIGHER EDUCATION STUDENTS BY FAMILY INCOME
(percentage of total enrollment)

Country and year	Students from top 20 percent of households by income
Chile, 1987	63[a]
Colombia, 1979	67
India, 1987	45
Indonesia, 1989	92
Japan, 1987	46
Malaysia, 1979	48
United States, 1987	37
Venezuela, 1986	77

a. Top 25 percent of households by income.
Sources: Tilak 1989, 1994; World Bank 1993c, 1993e.

FIGURE 3.4. PUBLIC EDUCATION EXPENDITURE AS A SHARE OF GNP AND OF CENTRAL
GOVERNMENT EXPENDITURE, 1980 AND 1990

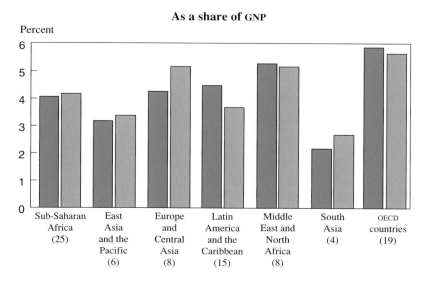

As a share of GNP

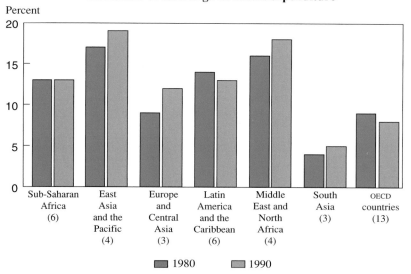

As a share of central government expenditure

◼ 1980   ◻ 1990

Note: Percentages are unweighted averages. Figures in parentheses refer to the number of countries in the
regional sample.
Sources: IMF and UNESCO databases.

TABLE 3.5   ALLOCATION OF EDUCATION BENEFITS IN EAST ASIA, 1985

Economy	Public expenditure on education as a share of GNP	Public expenditure on primary and secondary education as a share of GNP	Share of education budget allocated to higher education	Share of education budget allocated to primary and secondary education
Hong Kong	2.8	1.9	25	69
Indonesia	2.3	2.0	9	89
Korea, Rep. of	3.0	2.5	10	84
Malaysia	7.9	5.9	15	75
Singapore	5.0	3.2	31	65
Thailand	3.2	2.6	12	81

Source: World Bank 1993a.

differences in the pattern of fee-charging. Countries in Africa, the Middle East, and Eastern Europe and Central Asia have little or no tradition of cost recovery in higher education. In half of all Asian countries, however, and in a fifth of Latin American ones, cost recovery accounts for more than 10 percent of recurrent expenditures in public higher education (World Bank 1994e).

The Potential for Increased Efficiency and Equity

Increasing public spending on education is not necessary in many cases because of the enormous potential of efficiency gains at current levels. This can be seen through a simple comparison of regions. Public spending on education in Africa, which has the lowest enrollment ratios of any region, represents a greater share of GNP (4.2 percent) than in East Asia (3.4 percent) and Latin America (3.7 percent), where primary education is nearly universal (see the top panel of figure 3.4). By 1990 an average 6-year-old in East Asia or in the Middle East and North Africa region could expect to complete over nine years of school. Yet public spending on education by countries in the Middle East and North Africa represented 5.2 percent of GNP, compared with only 3.4 percent in East Asia. Some, but not most, of the difference is accounted for by demographic structure.

There is no theoretically appropriate proportion of GNP or public spending that should be devoted to education. In many countries, however, more educational attainment could be achieved with the same or even less public spending, particularly by following the East Asian pattern of focusing public spending on the lower levels of education and increasing its internal efficiency (table 3.5)

**FIGURE 3.5   RELATION BETWEEN PUBLIC SPENDING ON EDUCATION AND GROSS
ENROLLMENT RATIOS FOR POPULATION AGES 6–23, SELECTED COUNTRIES, 1990**

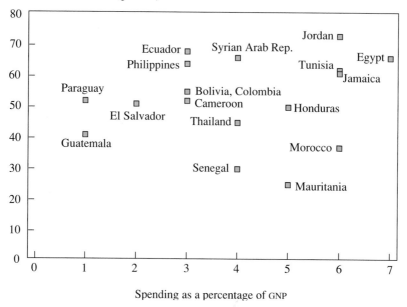

Gross enrollment ratio (percent)

Spending as a percentage of GNP

Source: Mingat and Tan 1994.

while relying more on private financing at the higher levels. Figure 3.5 compares public spending on education as a percentage of GNP with gross enrollment ratios for a sample of countries. While net enrollment ratios would be a better measure, such an international comparison using gross ratios does help identify countries where public spending appears to stimulate relatively low levels of human capital formation. Mauritania and Morocco, for instance, show particularly poor results despite high levels of public spending on education; their public spending on education is very inefficient compared with that of Jamaica, Jordan, and Tunisia. Similarly, Senegal and Thailand are inefficient compared with Syria.

Such comparisons also show that public spending is very low in some countries compared with international averages. In Paraguay, for instance, public spending appears to be relatively efficient compared with spending in Colombia and Thailand, which have the same outcomes but devote more than twice the share of GNP to public spending on education. Paraguay could probably increase educational attainment by spending more public funds on education.

Financing Education

The often-encountered inefficiencies and inequities of public expenditure on education have combined with expanding public sector enrollments at all levels to increase the share of GNP of public spending on education in many regions, particularly since unit costs are higher for secondary and tertiary students than for primary students. (The exceptions in shares spent are Latin America and the Middle East.) This trend has frequently put increasing pressure on public funds at the same time as many countries, especially in Eastern Europe and Africa, have experienced general fiscal difficulties. Indeed some countries' macroeconomic difficulties have in part been driven by fiscal problems resulting from education spending. In Kenya, for instance, spending on education rose from 30 percent of the government budget in 1980 to almost 40 percent by 1990, largely because admissions to public universities quadrupled.

During the 1980s public spending on education increased or maintained its share of GNP and increased as a share of total central government spending in every region of the developing world, except in Latin America with its debt-induced recession (see figure 3.4). Even more significant than total spending is spending per student, although such data are particularly limited in availability and reliability. Real public expenditure per student fell at the primary level not only in seven of the nine Latin American countries for which data are available but also in thirteen of twenty African countries. Real spending per student fell at the secondary level in Africa as well, by 18 percent. At the tertiary level, rapidly increasing enrollments in the 1980s combined with falling recurrent expenditure resulted in a decline in real per student expenditure (figure 3.6), with a particularly acute fall in Africa of 34 percent. Among OECD countries, by contrast, all but one of the fourteen for which data are available increased real expenditure per student at both the primary and secondary levels during the 1980s, and half increased spending at the tertiary level (Donors to African Education 1994; UNESCO database).

Measures to increase the efficiency of public spending on education can release funds for more productive investment in education. The share of higher education in central and state government spending in India, for instance, fell from 21 to 19 percent between 1976 and 1991, although primary education remains underfunded at 48 percent compared with secondary at 33 percent. Such reallocations may still not be enough, and other sources of funds may be required, particularly when overall public spending is falling. In Burkina Faso, for instance, the share of education spending devoted to primary education

FIGURE 3.6　GROWTH OF ENROLLMENT IN AND PUBLIC EXPENDITURE ON HIGHER
EDUCATION BY INCOME GROUP, 1980–88

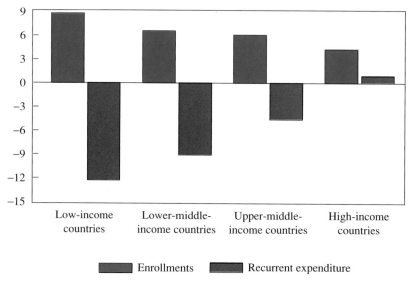

Average annual change (percent)

Enrollments　　　Recurrent expenditure

Source: Salmi 1991.

increased from 23 to 42 percent between 1980 and 1990 but dropped in absolute terms, as spending fell from 2.9 to 2.3 percent of GNP. In these circumstances, some countries have chosen to switch further public expenditure into
education and away from other publicly funded activities, such as defense and
inefficient public enterprises that can be run better by the private sector. Other
countries have decided that their macroeconomic policies have the scope to
expand spending on education by increasing the revenues of government. Military spending in many developing countries exceeds that for education, having
quintupled in constant dollars between 1960 and 1991—twice the rate of increase of per capita income—and is only slightly less than the combined total
for both education and health spending (McNamara 1992). Uganda reduced its
defense spending from 3.8 percent of GNP in 1989 to 1.5 percent by 1992,
increasing education spending from 1.4 to 1.7 percent of GNP and health spending from 0.5 to 0.8 percent (World Bank 1994m). Several Indian states increased spending on education from about 2.5 percent of state domestic prod-

FIGURE 3.7   RELATION BETWEEN GROSS ENROLLMENT RATIOS IN HIGHER EDUCATION
AND EXTENT OF PRIVATE FINANCING, SELECTED ASIAN COUNTRIES, ABOUT 1985

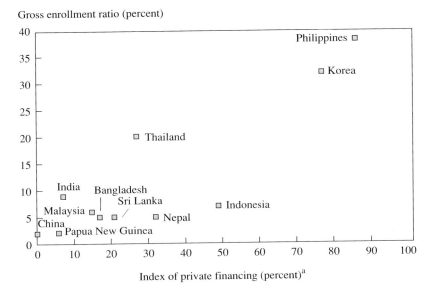

a. Reflects the rate of cost recovery across institutional types weighted by their share of total enrollments.
Source: Tan and Mingat 1992.

uct in the mid-1970s to more than 4 percent in 1990. Ghana increased its share
of education in public spending from 27 percent in 1984 to 36 percent in 1988.

Not all countries will be able to reallocate resources from, for example,
defense to education, or to raise revenues. Some countries have sought to
supplement public funds for education by injecting private funds. Private
funds can increase enrollments, whether they are used at private or at publicly
funded institutions. In Asia the more that higher education costs are financed
through student fees, the greater is the overall coverage of the education system
(figure 3.7).

The very existence of private schools and universities promotes diversity
and provides useful competition for public institutions, especially at the higher
levels of education. Some countries, however, prohibit private schools and
universities, and others regulate them excessively. Since private schools are
usually financed mainly by household payments of fees, such restrictions prevent private spending on education that could have substituted for public spend-

TABLE 3.6   GOVERNMENT AND HOUSEHOLD EXPENDITURE ON EDUCATION IN KENYA, BY LEVEL, 1992–93
(percentage of GDP)

Level	Government direct	Household direct	Deferred cost recovery [a]	Total
Primary	2.63	1.19	0	3.82
Secondary	0.78	1.26	0	2.04
Public university	0.79	0.06	0.14	0.99
Other/unallocated	0.37	1.99	0	2.36
Total	4.57	4.50	0.14	9.21

a. Student loan scheme.
Source: World Bank 1994g.

ing and permitted more students to enroll at publicly funded schools. In Iran, for instance, tertiary enrollments have expanded since the private Islamic Azad University was established in 1983 and now number more than 300,000, or 40 percent of higher education enrollments. Students at the university pay tuition; those at the public universities do not.

Charging fees for students at publicly funded institutions raises difficult questions concerning equity, efficiency, access, and taxation. If some fees are charged for all students attending public schools at all levels, the poor will be hit particularly hard, discouraging enrollment. Scholarship and other systems used to offset this blow are inherently very complex to administer at the lower levels of education. At the upper-secondary and higher levels there is a much stronger case for the payment of fees. The gap between the private and social returns to education is generally much greater in higher education than in basic education; that is, the subsidy to the student is larger compared with future earnings (see table 1.1). This inefficiency can be overcome by charging the student, either from current family income or from future earnings, by means of a loan scheme or through the tax system. Yet, too often household financing of education is concentrated more on the lower than on the higher levels. In Kenya, for instance, households absorb about 31 percent of the costs of primary education and 62 percent of those at secondary level but only about 20 percent of those in higher education (table 3.6).

CHAPTER FOUR

Improving Quality

THE QUALITY of education is defined by both the learning environment and student outcomes. A wide variety of policies and inputs, tailored to specific conditions, can bring about effective schooling. Although resource availability certainly affects quality, educational research and experience show that public sector policies and investments can influence the quality of education. The implications of these findings are not generally applied because of the prevailing patterns of education expenditure and management and the vested interests associated with them.

Education outcomes can be improved through four important actions: (a) setting standards for performance; (b) supporting inputs known to improve achievement; (c) adopting flexible strategies for the acquisition and use of inputs; and (d) monitoring performance. This chapter deals with the first three actions at the school level, principally in primary education. Monitoring performance, an essential complement to these three actions, is covered in chapter 6. Quality improvement at the higher level is usually handled through funding mechanisms (see chapter 10).

Setting Standards

Governments can improve academic achievement by setting clear learning objectives and high performance standards for core subjects. Standards have led to positive results in the school systems of such industrial countries as Australia, France, Germany, and Japan (Tuijnman and Postlethwaite 1994). Performance standards are important for all levels of education but have often been neglected at the primary level. In many countries standards at the secondary and tertiary levels are embodied in certification examinations.

Many countries are moving toward establishing performance standards at the primary level. For example, India has established minimal levels of learning for subject areas in each primary grade. In mathematics, students in class 1 are expected to be able to count from 1 to 20 using objects and pictures; the competent student in class 4 recognizes and writes numerals from 1,000 to 10,000 (NCERT 1994).

Effective performance standards reflect the consensus of professional educators, parents, and students and often involve the political process. Parents are best able to judge what knowledge and skills they wish schools to impart to their children, while professional educators can provide essential expertise concerning developmentally appropriate performance objectives and effective strategies for reaching these objectives. At the secondary and tertiary levels, students' demands for skills need to be taken into account. In most countries with effective systems of performance standards, consensus building is part of the process of setting standards. Jordan's education reform program, which originated with a general conference on educational development in 1987, included a participatory approach to the setting of national standards.

Standard setting may be a lengthy process in countries with heterogeneous populations and distinct regional and ethnic cultures. Careful delineation of core academic subjects as the focus for performance standard setting may help in resolving differences between groups. It is also important to guard against minimum standards becoming the maximum aimed for by teachers (Madaus and Greaney 1985)—as appears to have happened in the Philippines.

Support for Effective Inputs

Once learning objectives have been identified, the "technology" of learning comes into play. Learning requires five types of inputs:

- The student's capacity and motivation to learn

- The subject to be learned

- A teacher who knows and can teach the subject

- Time for learning

- The requisite tools for teaching and learning.

An extensive literature shows that interventions to increase learning opportunity provided by any of the inputs will contribute to the amount and speed of learning by a student, particularly at the primary and secondary levels and where initial levels of inputs are low (Lockheed, Verspoor, and others 1991). The literature also documents an enormous variety in the specifics of each type of input and how it can be provided, beginning with the home.

Students' Capacity and Motivation to Learn

Students' capacity and motivation to learn are determined by the quality of the home and school environments, the students' health and nutrition status, and their prior learning experiences, including the degree of parental stimulation. The principal source of children's capacity and motivation to learn is the family, through genetic endowment and the direct provision of nutrients, health care, and stimulus. For children whose families are unable to provide the necessary inputs, early childhood programs and school health and nutrition programs can provide substitutes. The long-run benefit of interventions during the preschool years are significant. Studies comparing the effects of school and family influences conclude that more than 60 percent of differences in student achievement can be attributed to differences in individual and family characteristics (Lombard 1994; Bryant and Ramey 1987; Schaeffer 1987; Schweinhart and Koshel 1986).

EARLY CHILDHOOD PROGRAMS. Programs that focus on the physical, cognitive and emotional development of young children increase the likelihood of their subsequent enrollment in school, improve their performance in school, and have wider benefits for the individual and society. Evidence from Brazil, India, Peru, Turkey, and the United States demonstrates that early childhood interventions can enhance school readiness and reduce dropout and repetition (Berg 1987; Chaturvedi and others 1987; Myers and others 1985; Kagitcibasi, Sunar, and Bekman 1987; Barnett 1992). The early years of life are crucial in the formation and development of intelligence, personality, and social behavior, and targeted integrated programs of health, nutrition, and cognitive stimulation can give disadvantaged children a better start in school. Early childhood programs need to monitor the child's health status, supply health and nutrition supplements when needed, and provide age-appropriate curricula, activities, and materials to encourage cognitive development. Programs should be so structured that every child receives attention every day. Parental and community involvement should be promoted (Young 1994). World Bank–assisted projects are beginning to include such programs. In Colombia, for instance, a project helps women repair and renovate their homes so that they can offer childcare facilities for the community. A project in Bolivia helps expand home-based day care in poor urban and periurban areas, and one in Mexico supports a program of parental education targeted to rural and indigenous poor in the states with the lowest per capita incomes. In India health, nutrition, and early education services are provided to more than 12 million children between 6 months and 6 years of age.

NUTRITION AND HEALTH PROGRAMS. Temporary hunger, chronic malnutrition, micronutrient deficiencies, parasitic infections, and vision and hearing impairments reduce a child's ability to achieve in school (Levinger 1992; Pollitt 1990). Most children with a history of malnutrition and poor health, it is now known, are capable of successful school performance if measures are taken to compensate for their deficiencies. (Severe health and nutrition deficiencies that inflict gross changes in the brain or irreversible physical damage cannot be so simply handled.) For many of the poor nutrition and health conditions affecting children, there are effective, safe, and relatively inexpensive interventions. Where costs are higher, interventions can be targeted to the needy poor.

Schoolchildren who suffer concurrent malnutrition and poor health perform less well and attend less regularly, leading to grade repetition or dropout. School-based vitamin A, iron, and iodine supplementation and mass delivery of deworming drugs through schools are perhaps the most cost-effective ways of improving children's readiness to learn via improved nutrition and health. These remedies are inexpensive, and providers do not require medical training, although distribution and logistical infrastructure do need to be well developed. Per child per year, deworming costs less than $1.50; vitamin A supplementation, less than $0.50; ferrous sulfate tablets for iron deficiency, between $2.00 and $4.00; and oral iodine supplementation, less than $0.50 (Bundy and others 1990; World Bank 1994c). Integration of programs can reduce costs further, and education programs designed to change specific nutrition and health practices or to increase knowledge among schoolchildren can complement and sustain these shorter-term interventions.

Children with impaired vision and hearing can be identified at negligible cost with the use of simple eye charts and whisper tests. Glasses and hearing aids could then be provided, or teachers could at least seat the children near the front of the room or take other helpful measures.

Temporary hunger affects the child's ability to pay attention and so has a detrimental effect on learning. Many governments support large and expensive school feeding programs. Such programs can be made more cost-effective by targeting them to the poor, by providing breakfast or snacks before school rather than a larger meal later in the day, and by selecting fortified foods or foods high in essential micronutrients.

Increasingly, World Bank–assisted projects are being designed to improve the quality of primary education through school nutrition and health interventions. A project in Brazil supports improvements in the school feeding program, screening of schoolchildren for health and nutrition status, the integration of health and nutrition instruction into the curriculum, and pilot programs for school-based vitamin A and iron supplementation. A project in Guinea is developing a national deworming and iodine supplementation program through the schools. Another, in the Dominican Republic, is assisting the implementation of a school snack program in poor urban areas, a national height census of first-graders, a micronutrient deficiency survey, and pilot school-based iron and vitamin A supplementation programs.

CURRICULUM. The curriculum defines the subjects to be taught and furnishes general guidance regarding the frequency and duration of instruction. In some cases an accompanying syllabus specifies more precisely what is to be taught and what will be assessed. Curricula and syllabi should be closely linked to performance standards and measures of outcome. The curriculum typically includes fewer subjects at lower levels and more subjects at higher ones. At the primary level there are broad international similarities in the relative emphasis placed on approximately eight major subjects; reading, writing, and mathematics account for about 50 percent of curricular emphasis (Benavot and Kamens 1989). Within each subject, the coverage, sequencing, and pacing of topics may vary widely between and within countries. At the secondary level countries differ with respect to the number of subjects taught, the balance between general and vocational subjects, the designation of mandatory and elective subjects, and the sequencing of subjects.

The range of national variation among relatively successful education systems shows clearly that no single curriculum is appropriate to all or most low- and middle-income countries. Intended variation between and within countries results from differences in desired outcomes, in theories of instruction, and in local conditions. These differences can affect which subjects are taught, when they are introduced, and how long they are taught. For example, schools in Burundi offer relatively fewer hours of instruction and more emphasis on language and mathematics than do schools in Kenya, where the school year is longer and the curriculum covers more subjects, with an emphasis on science (Eisemon and Schwille 1991; Eisemon, Schwille, and Prouty 1989). In Japan finite mathematics, including statistics, is introduced in grade 6 and precalculus and calculus in grades 7–9; in the United States these subjects are taught in grades 11 and 12.

Another type of curricular variation is unintended: the discrepancy between the official curriculum and the one actually implemented in schools and classrooms. This variation has two main causes. The first is technical: in many countries educational systems, schools, and classrooms are unable to deliver the key ingredients for learning: a teacher who can teach the subject, time for learning, and the requisite tools for teaching and learning. Second, competing incentives (or disincentives) can affect the number of hours teachers or students spend in school and the attention paid to specific subjects. Opportunity costs of student and teacher time are the most important disincentive to maintaining official norms for instructional time. Student dropout in Ghana was highest when the direct and indirect costs to the family for children's school participation were highest—the direct costs were highest during famine times and the indirect costs during peak agricultural seasons. In Jamaica, student absenteeism is highest on market days. Teacher absenteeism can result when teachers hold multiple jobs or have to commute long distances to their assigned schools. Selection examinations provide strong incentives for ignoring certain subjects in favor of the subjects that are tested. For example, in Jamaica students in grades 5 and 6 spend a disproportionate amount of time studying vocabulary lists and mathematics problems in preparation for the Common Entrance Examination for secondary-level schooling, to the detriment of subjects in the primary curriculum that are not tested on that examination.

Children's gender-role development is affected by many aspects of the school environment, such as curricula and instructional materials. While most countries have a national curriculum meant to expose boys and girls to the same subjects, gender-differentiated courses are still offered in many schools. Boys tend to outnumber girls in mathematics, science, and mechanical courses, while the reverse is true for homemaking courses in many countries. Girls may consequently perform poorly on quantitative tests, discouraging expectations of academic achievement (Martin and Levy 1994). A heavy bias in the curricula toward low-paying skills for females, such as sewing, knitting, and secretarial work, can also strongly influence girls' future employment opportunities by limiting women's access to better-paying jobs (Herz and others 1991).

Textbooks and other educational materials in many countries have been found to have a pronounced gender bias that portrays women as admiring, passive, and powerless, suited for traditional roles only. In contrast, men are depicted as intelligent and capable of employment in a great number of exciting and profitable fields (box 4.1). These messages can reinforce negative stereotypes, discouraging girls from viewing themselves as good students, as intelligent, or as capable of pursuing any occupations other than a few traditional ones (Herz and others 1991).

Many primary curricula include too many subjects, reducing the time available for teaching core language and number skills. Furthermore, many curricula require the teaching of several languages (the native language, the

BOX 4.1. GENDER BIAS IN TEXTBOOKS

Since the mid-1970s parental pressure on publishers has led to reduction of gender bias in textbooks in industrial countries, but in developing countries relatively little change has occurred (Stromquist 1994). A study in Zambia revealed that while textbooks systematically treated the activities of men as admirable, women, if featured at all, were portrayed in domestic roles and depicted as stupid, ignorant, and passive (Hyde 1989). An analysis of government and commercial textbooks in Costa Rica in 1985 found that 75 percent of the images were of males and 25 percent of females. Males were commonly shown as historical figures, in pursuit of intellectual activity or working in agriculture and ranching, while females were usually shown doing domestic tasks and caring for children. In one story a poor female street vendor drops her basket of wares while thinking of plans for the future. The accompanying text—"What should the woman have been doing instead of imagining future possibilities?"—implies negative consequences of women's imagination. Costa Rica has since introduced a new series of books in an effort to reduce gender bias (González-Suárez 1987; Lockheed, Verspoor, and others 1991). Such discrepancies in the representation of men and women in textbooks have been found across regions and cultures in, for example, Colombia, Egypt, India, Kuwait, Lebanon, Qatar, Saudi Arabia, Tunisia, and Yemen (Lockheed, Verspoor, and others 1991; Stromquist 1994).

---

national or regional language of instruction, the metropolitan language, and so on). Learning is more effective, and time is saved, if instruction in the first several grades is in the child's native language. This approach allows for mastery of the first language and promotes the cognitive development needed for learning a second language (Dutcher 1994). Once solid skills in the first language have been acquired, a national, regional, or metropolitan language can be learned in the later primary grades to prepare for secondary education. Production of textbooks in native languages may, however, increase the costs of education.

"Language capital"—the ability to speak, read, or write one or more languages—is an important aspect of human capital. Building up language capital begins early, with the development of oral fluency in one's native language. The development of language capital in the native language continues in school and elsewhere. The native language of most poor minority groups, however, is not the majority or dominant language spoken in the country. Not knowing the dominant language may limit a person's training opportunities, job mobility, and earnings and reduce that person's chances of escaping poverty. There is, therefore, a labor-market incentive for acquiring skills in the dominant language (Chiswick 1991; Chiswick and Miller 1995).

Whereas the primary education curriculum is relatively standard across countries, secondary education curricula vary in duration (from two to six years), in the use of residential programs, in differentiation by streams (science, teacher training, vocational, and so on), and in the number of courses offered (from 10 to 200). Science education and vocational education raise particularly complex issues because of their perceived importance and their cost.

Science education is important for economic development and is increasingly incorporated in the curriculum. Advanced science education requires expensive laboratories and equipment, and teacher training in these subjects is costly. Many countries view all science education at the lower- and upper-secondary levels as "advanced" and restrict access to science education. In the Philippines, for example, science is offered only at special schools. Yet, as OECD countries are recognizing, laboratory-based instruction is not essential for science education at primary or lower-secondary levels. Once laboratory use is reduced or eliminated, the costs of science education are no longer significantly higher than those of other subjects, as evidence from Denmark shows. This means that instruction in a core subject need not be restricted because of expense. Students at lower levels still need to work with simple concrete objects and to see charts because they need more help with conceptualizing than do older students.

Vocational and technical skills are best imparted in the workplace, following general education. The private sector should be directly involved in the provision, financing, and governance of vocational schooling. At the secondary level, vocational education and general education are converging, as such subjects as science, technology, mathematics, and English are added to the vocational curriculum and as general secondary education increasingly includes basic technological education. This convergence has yet to be evaluated in terms of labor market outcomes. It is, however, in harmony with the trend toward rapidly changing labor markets that place an increased emphasis on trainability. It is also consistent with earlier comparisons which showed clearly that the social rates of return to investment in very specialized vocational secondary education were lower than those to general secondary education, largely because of the much higher costs of the former (Psacharopoulos 1989).

Curriculum reform policies typically focus on changing the intended curriculum: the types of courses to be offered, the level at which they are to be introduced, and their duration. For example, Malawi introduces health education as early as grade 2, and Kenya's curricular and structural reform of the mid-1980s introduced several new subjects, raising to thirteen the number to be examined at the end of the new primary cycle. However, curriculum reforms that focus on revisions of courses and timetables without concomitant revisions in standards and guidelines, instructional materials, teaching practice, and the incentives offered by tests and examinations are likely to have little impact.

Many countries have adopted a two-pronged approach to curricular reform. First, performance standards for learning are established and outcomes are measured through examinations or national assessments. Second, within the general curriculum, local variation in the use of materials, in teaching methods, and in the allocation of time is encouraged. Kenya, for instance, has a national curriculum, but schools determine the language of instruction in the first four primary grades. India's Department of Education has developed a competency-based curriculum around the concept of minimal levels of learning, but states and districts are responsible for adapting materials and teacher training to local conditions.

What Are the Necessary Inputs?

A wide variety of policies and practices, chosen to fit local circumstances, can bring about effective schooling. In low- and middle-income countries school and classroom characteristics account for only about 40 percent of differences in learning achievement; the remainder, as noted earlier, is attributable to individual and family-background characteristics not typically amenable to school-level interventions.

Recent reviews of the literature on correlates of learning in low- and middle-income countries show that the most consistently positive effects are found for teacher subject knowledge, instructional time, textbooks, and instructional materials (Fuller and Clarke 1994; Lockheed, Verspoor, and others 1991; Harbison and Hanushek 1992; Velez, Schiefelbein, and Valenzuela 1993). Inputs in these categories would have the highest priority for expenditure. However, the exact composition of the basket of inputs and their relative importance for a given school will vary widely in accordance with local conditions. For example, a recent study of reading achievement in twenty-five countries (Postlethwaite and Ross 1992) found that of fifty-six inputs examined, only eleven contributed to learning in at least three of the four developing countries included (Hungary, Indonesia, Trinidad and Tobago, and Venezuela).

In many countries, education systems have made a practice of investing in inputs that expand access (for example, hiring more teachers to reduce class size) instead of those that have a demonstrable effect on enhancing learning (Hanushek 1994). Such inputs as smaller classes and higher teacher salaries set on the basis of seniority and formal qualifications are cited less often in the research literature, however, and therefore probably deserve lower priority (figure 4.1). In addition, expensive inputs, such as laboratories, are not effective.

FIGURE 4.1   DETERMINANTS OF EFFECTIVE LEARNING AT THE PRIMARY LEVEL

Percentage of studies showing positive effect

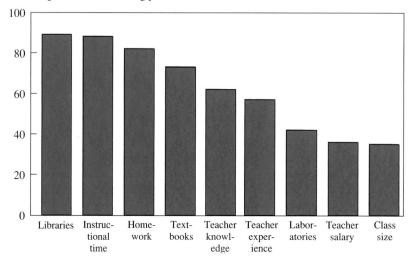

Note: Studies covered more than twenty-five countries.
Source: Fuller and Clarke 1994.

TEACHERS' KNOWLEDGE AND SKILLS. Teachers' subject knowledge, an intended outcome of preservice training, is strongly and consistently related to
student performance. Teachers with a better knowledge of subject material and
greater written and verbal language proficiency have better-performing students (Lockheed, Verspoor, and others 1991; Harbison and Hanushek 1992, for
Brazil; Ross and Postlethwaite 1989, for Indonesia; Warwick and Reimers
1992, for Pakistan; Bashir 1994, for India). In both Brazil and Pakistan, teachers' own subject knowledge and formal education had more impact on student
performance than did preservice training (Warwick and Reimers 1992). At the
primary level, research suggests that the overall level of relevant knowledge
is insufficient in many countries. For example, in India less than half of grade
4 teachers could correctly answer 80 percent of questions testing grade 4
mathematics knowledge (Bashir 1994). The curriculum for preservice education may need to be revised to stress knowledge of the subject matter. Related
to teachers' subject knowledge is their pedagogical knowledge. Although no
specific teaching practice is universally effective, teachers with a wide reper-

toire of teaching skills appear to be more effective than those with a limited repertoire.

The most effective strategy for ensuring that teachers have adequate subject knowledge is to recruit suitably educated teachers whose knowledge has been assessed. The assessment of learning outcomes for higher education—including teacher education—is as important as it is for the primary and secondary levels. In fact, subject matter knowledge is routinely tested for secondary and tertiary teachers but not for primary teachers. There are a few exceptions, such as Mexico, where teacher knowledge is related to pay at all levels of education. Harbison and Hanushek (1992) suggest a national teacher examination, based on their findings for Brazil and other countries. At a minimum, the recruitment of primary and secondary teachers could resemble more the recruitment of higher education teachers, which is almost entirely based on subject knowledge—as in France and Japan, where recruitment is highly selective.

Well-designed, continuous in-service training is a second strategy for improving teacher subject knowledge and related pedagogical practices. Recognized effective elements of in-service training include exposure to new theory or techniques, demonstrations of their application, practice by the teacher, feedback to the teacher, and coaching over time (Joyce and Showers 1985, 1987, 1988; Joyce, Hersh, and McKibbin 1983; Joyce 1991). As these elements suggest, in-service training is most effective when it is linked directly to classroom practice by the teacher (Walberg 1991; Nitsaisook and Anderson 1989) and provided by the head teacher (Raudenbush, Bhumirat, and Kamali 1989). The effect of in-service training on student achievement has been demonstrated for the Escuela Nueva program in Colombia (Colbert, Chiappe, and Arboleda 1993), for science in the Philippines (Lockheed, Fonacier, and Bianchi 1989), and for mathematics in Botswana (Fuller, Hua, and Snyder 1994). Distance education programs for in-service (and preservice) teacher training are typically more cost-effective than residential programs. For example, in Sri Lanka distance education programs of up to four years in duration are more than five times as cost-effective as two-year programs in colleges of education or in teachers' colleges (Nielsen and Tatto 1991). In Botswana in-service training is a more efficient way to raise achievement than reducing class size or providing supplementary reading materials (Fuller, Hua, and Snyder 1994).

TIME. The amount of actual time for learning is consistently related to achievement. More time spent on a wider coverage of the curriculum results in increased learning and less variation among achievement levels (Stevenson and Baker 1991; McKnight 1971). Internationally the school year averages 880 hours per year of instruction at the primary level. The official primary school year is shorter in low- and middle-income countries than in industrial countries, however. In addition, students in low- and middle-income countries spend much less time being instructed than those in OECD countries as a consequence of unscheduled school closings, teacher and student absences, and miscellaneous disruptions (Lockheed, Verspoor, and others 1991).

The first strategy for increasing the amount of instructional time is to increase the length of the official school year, if it falls significantly below the norm. There is no guarantee, however, that schools will implement the official school year, particularly if it makes no accommodation for local conditions that may affect the participation of teachers or students. In many countries, schools or regions are permitted flexible scheduling of the instructional day, week, or year to accommodate variations in demand associated with weather, agricultural seasons, religious holidays, and children's domestic chores. This strategy has been effective in both nonformal programs of basic education and formal programs supported by the World Bank in Bangladesh, Colombia, Costa Rica, and Ecuador. A second strategy for increasing learning time is to assign homework—an approach that has been effective in OECD countries.

TOOLS AND TECHNOLOGY. Instructional materials include the entire range of teaching tools, from chalk to computers. After blackboards and chalk, textbooks are the most common and most significant instructional material in most countries. The availability of teaching tools at all levels in low- and middle-income countries is limited, particularly at the primary level. In some countries textbooks are supplemented by libraries, other print and graphics materials, audiocassettes, films, radios, television, and computers (Lockheed, Middleton, and Nettleton 1991). Particularly critical in improving reading achievement is the provision of supplementary reading material, since voluntary reading and library usage, together with teacher education, are correlated with reading achievement (Lundberg and Linnakyla 1992; Postlethwaite and Ross 1992). Hence the importance of libraries in figure 4.1.

Almost all studies of textbooks in low- and middle-income countries show that the books have a positive impact on student achievement (Heyneman, Farrell, and Sepulveda-Stuardo 1978; Fuller and Clarke 1994). In addition, interactive radio instruction has been found to have a positive and cost-effective impact on mathematics, science, and English achievement at the primary level in Bolivia, Honduras, Lesotho, and Papua New Guinea (Tilson 1991).

New technologies stand to improve the efficiency of education through software tools that improve student performance and through new means of providing instruction and educational resources to underserved populations. Computers improve student achievement and attitudes at all levels (Thompson, Simonson, and Hargrave 1992), and small-scale experiments with computer-based instruction have been carried out in several low- and middle-income countries, including Chile, Mexico, and the Philippines. In industrial countries technologies are being innovatively combined at the primary and secondary levels to increase instructional effectiveness. Intelligent tutoring systems, CD-ROM, multimedia, and other applications have improved student achievement in all disciplines (Sivin-Kachala and Bialo 1994), from early childhood programs through college preparatory classes. Broadcast and network technologies allow teachers with specialized skills (such as Japanese or Russian language teachers) and educational resources (such as on-line libraries) to reach beyond the traditional limits of classrooms and schools. Teachers can reach students via interactive television, teleconferencing, computer conferencing, audiographics, voice and data transmission systems, shared electronic blackboards and light pens, fax, voice-mail, computer bulletin boards, and electronic mail. Transmission systems include satellites, microwave, fiber-optics, interactive cable systems, and microcomputers connected to local and international networks.

At the tertiary level technology can substitute, at least partially, for teachers. Correspondence courses and open universities, for example, can increase cost-effectiveness. Satellite and computer technology allow high-quality interactive courses to be broadcast directly to places of work, in cooperation with firms that wish to improve their employees' skills. Students can save significant travel time to and from school and do not forgo income by interrupting employment to earn a more advanced degree. For example, in the United States the National Technological University (NTU) offers 1,000 master's degree courses annually via satellite to over 100,000 regular and continuing education students. NTU's unique learning consortium includes 43 accredited universities and over 200 firms (National Technological University 1994). This model is being copied to provide distance instruction in both industrial and developing countries.

Even in industrial countries, many programs using educational technology are still in the pilot stage and depend on grant funding. Initial costs are generally high, and the costs of adding additional users are low, but all costs are closely linked to the idiosyncrasies of individual technologies and to the quality and availability of local telecommunications infrastructure. As a rule, these programs depend on reliable, high-quality telecommunications connections (Derfler 1992), which are seldom found in developing countries. Even where programs are technically feasible, low- and middle-income countries may lack the experienced pedagogical and technical support necessary for successful implementation. The need to use scarce resources for other instructional materials and for the improvement of existing educational programs, combined with lack of institutional support and of information about appropriate, durable, and cost-effective technologies, has limited the widespread use of advanced educational technology in many low- and middle-income countries. Failure fully to use this technology carries the risk of further increasing the gap between these countries and industrial ones.

The World Bank has supported governments in their efforts to design, print and distribute textbooks "in-house." World Bank projects now routinely include funding for textbooks, which accounted for 6 percent of all education lending in fiscal 1990–94, compared with 3 percent a decade earlier. Support for textbooks is now broken down into development, production, distribution, and use. Textbook development needs to be closely linked with curriculum development. Production and distribution are best handled by the private sector, although governments need assistance with procurement policies and with measures for ensuring quality. The effective use of textbooks must involve training teachers in the use of new books and providing teacher guides. Some governments have also provided packages of instructional materials, such as wall charts, games, anatomic models, and science kits. In Mexico, for example, such packages have been provided under two consecutive World Bank–assisted primary education projects; the packages prepared under the second project were modified on the basis of experience with the first project.

Flexibility in Providing Inputs

Setting standards and supporting effective inputs are important for raising learning achievement. Even more critical is the flexibility to decide locally how to combine and manage inputs in schools and other educational institutions. Governments can support this flexibility through their method of providing inputs and by encouraging the conditions that have been shown to promote student learning. Governments have principally employed two strategies for providing inputs to schools and institutions of higher education, and the World Bank has supported both. The first strategy has been direct provision of packages of inputs. Experience shows that centrally provided packages are not used unless the inputs fit local conditions, teachers know how to use the inputs, and policies related to the use of inputs do not act as disincentives. The second strategy has been to provide budget transfers so that schools and other institutions can purchase what is most relevant to prevailing local conditions.

No single package of inputs can be considered "most effective" or most cost-effective for all schools or all preexisting conditions, and it is difficult to specify in advance what will work in a particular situation. School personnel have the closest knowledge of preexisting conditions and are in the best position to select the most suitable package of inputs. Even when school personnel have not been delegated authority for budgets, their knowledge can be employed to tailor packages of inputs to local conditions. In Jamaica the World Bank is supporting a comprehensive reform of secondary education that includes curriculum revision for grades 7–9, teacher training in curriculum objectives, provision of tools and technology for curriculum implementation, and assessment of student learning in the core curriculum areas. Before receiving a package of instructional materials for the core curriculum subject, school personnel complete an inventory of materials already available in the school, and only the missing materials are provided. The results are significant cost savings over the alternative of providing all schools with all materials.

In some countries schools have authority in curriculum choices and textbook selection but not over budgets and personnel. In most high-income countries teachers and schools select books from an approved list. This practice is gradually being introduced elsewhere, notably in the transition economies of Europe and Central Asia. In only a few cases do school-level personnel have full autonomy, with authority in all the critical aspects of school management: budget, curriculum, and personnel. Even this practice does not necessarily lead to higher student achievement, however. Preliminary evaluations of school-based management in the United States and Canada do not demonstrate any effect—positive or negative—of this reform on achievement (Summers and Johnson 1994; GAO 1994). A more promising approach, tested so far only in industrial countries, is school-based leadership that ensures an effective climate for learning (box 4.2). Even easier to achieve is the appointment of the best

---

BOX 4.2. A PROMISING AVENUE: SCHOOL LEADERSHIP

School characteristics that are important for achievement center on each school's leadership. Effective learning institutions in industrial countries have leadership able to ensure that resources are available, to communicate a vision for the school that includes high expectations for students and an orderly environment, and to provide pedagogic guidance and support to teachers. This support may not require full autonomy over budgets, curriculum, and personnel.

Pedagogic leadership at the institutional level needs to support the classroom conditions that are known to foster learning. Students whose teachers have high expectations for their students and offer rewards and incentives for academic achievement learn more. When teaching methods respond to the behavioral and learning styles of students and when classes are disciplined so that learning time is high, student achievement is usually higher.

Governments can foster school leadership and classroom conditions which encourage learning by ensuring that these factors are prominent in the selection and training of teachers, school principals, and administrators and that they are central objectives of school supervision, inspection, and support activities (Brookover and Lezotte 1979; Brubaker and Partine 1986; Carter and Klotz 1990; Chubb and Moe 1990; Dalin 1992; Frederick 1987; Gibbs 1989; Hallinger 1989; Joyce, Hersh, and McKibbin 1983; Levine 1990; Levine and Lezotte 1990; Lezotte and others 1980; Lezotte and Bancroft 1985; Purkey and Smith 1983; Scheerens and Creemers 1989; Smith and Andrews 1989; Steller 1988; Wynne 1980).

principals to the neediest schools, such as rural multigrade schools and those in urban slums.

Many education systems in low- and middle-income countries are rigid, run in a centralized manner with, for instance, central selection and purchase of textbooks and central direction concerning classroom instruction. Despite this, many schools have considerable de facto autonomy, at least about the method of instruction, if not about the deployment of teaching staff. However, management and supervisory links are often weak, and teachers work in isolation, especially in small schools. The consequence of this isolation is that the curriculum is not implemented, instructional time is reduced, and teaching tools are not used. Three factors are necessary for overcoming these shortcomings: shared local consensus about desired outcomes, professionalism among teachers, and school autonomy. These three factors combine to hold the school and its teachers accountable to parents and communities for outcomes in the context of national or regional indicators of performance, such as examinations and learning assessments.

PART II

Six Key Reforms

THE EDUCATION challenges described in chapter 2 can be met if reforms are introduced along the lines of the changes in the financing and management of education discussed in chapters 3 and 4. Six reforms, taken together, will go a long way toward enabling low- and middle-income countries to meet the challenges in access, equity, quality, and pace of reform that they face today. These reforms are a higher priority for education; attention to outcomes; concentration of efficient public investment on basic education, coupled with more reliance on household financing for higher education; attention to equity; household involvement in the education system; and autonomous institutions that will permit the flexible combination of instructional inputs.

Since education challenges are present to varying degrees in individual countries, the six reforms will not all have the same priority everywhere. And, while much of the discussion necessarily involves the setting of subsectoral priorities, it must never be forgotten that the education system is indeed a system and that changes and investments in one subsector will have implications for other subsectors and for the system as a whole.

The six key reforms called for in this report will help to improve education and, in the poorer countries, to reduce illiteracy in the future. They will not, however, contribute significantly to solving the problem of adult illiteracy today, in a world with more than 900 million illiterates. Programs of adult education are necessary, but such programs have a poor track record. One study showed an effectiveness rate of just 13 percent for adult literacy campaigns conducted over the past thirty years (Abadzi 1994), and there has been little research into the benefits and costs of literacy programs. Several new approaches to adult literacy appear promising, however, in large part because they address motivation—the key factor in all successful programs. Adult literacy efforts have a better chance of success if they (a) have an initial objective other than literacy, such as reading sacred literature like the Koran, acquiring health information, or assisting with children's education; (b) distinguish among teenagers and older adults, as adults learn in different ways from adolescents; (c) include women as well as men (most unsuccessful campaigns have focused on male themes); and (d) use a participatory pedagogy sensitive to the local environment. In the REFLECT program, being developed with the help of the NGO ActionAid in Bangladesh, El Salvador, and Uganda, poor communities are encouraged to construct maps, calendars, matrices, and diagrams based on local circumstances and are helped to analyze and systematize their knowledge. The alphabet and literacy then become a more elaborate way of representing this local knowledge, and literacy is linked much more tightly to other aspects of development in the local area. These new approaches will be reviewed in detail in a future World Bank paper, prompted by challenges to the view that large-scale literacy programs are generally unsuccessful. The paper will also analyze the costs and benefits of literacy programs and the factors that were important in the successful implementation of programs that have been expanded from small experiments to the national level. This issue is not further discussed in this report, which focuses on mainstream formal education.

CHAPTER FIVE

A Higher Priority for Education

GOVERNMENTS and peoples in almost all countries need to pay more attention to education. Education is usually the province of the ministry of education—sometimes also of a ministry of higher education—and other parts of government tend to leave it to this body. This method is short-sighted, for three reasons.

- Continuous change in economies and labor markets is now normal, as the result of permanent economic reform and technological change that necessitate renewed and enduring attention to investment in both physical and human capital.

- The rate of return to investments in education is high compared with other investments.

- There are important synergies among investments in education and other aspects of human capital formation, especially nutrition, health, and fertility.

During the 1980s and early 1990s many countries began restructuring their economies, driven by macroeconomic imbalances, excessive external debt, and an increasingly competitive world economy. Economic reform programs have now brought positive results in the two regions where they were most necessary; economic growth has resumed in both Africa and Latin America. African countries have made much progress in many key areas of macroeconomic reform, but these efforts must be sustained and expanded, especially to include the achievement of fiscal balance. Increasing international trade and the increasing mobility of capital and technology have made most economies more open and have created a more competitive environment for attracting global investment. China and India are the two largest examples of countries with increasingly competitive and open economies. (The record of East Asia was discussed in chapter 1.) Developments in the transition economies of Europe and Asia are even more dramatic, as wholesale shifts toward market economic structures occur.

Now that economic reform is becoming a permanent process, it is important for governments to focus on the factors, in addition to appropriate macroeconomic policies, that are necessary for sustaining growth and reducing poverty. Investment in production and services is increasingly attracted to countries with the necessary physical infrastructure and with flexible labor forces. All governments must pay renewed attention to investment in infrastructure and to investment in people if they are to stimulate private sector investment and hence growth. The appropriate physical infrastructure and human capital investments will vary from country to country according to the level of economic and educational development. Investment in people is particularly critical because of the lags between investments in education and the entry of new workers into the labor force. Delays in reforming education systems therefore carry the risk of reducing future economic growth.

Investments in all levels of education yield high rates of return—above the opportunity cost of capital, which is usually thought to be around 8–10 percent, and comparable to (or, for lower levels of education, higher than) the rates of return to investments in agriculture, industry, and infrastructure (table 5.1). Moreover, these social rates of return to education are underestimates because they exclude benefits such as improved health and reduced fertility, as well as external economies such as threshold effects and technology acquisition and development. Investments in physical and human capital investment are complementary; without investments in education, investments in physical capital will yield lower returns, and vice versa.

Increased understanding of the relationships among education, nutrition, health, and fertility warrants greater attention to education. Parents, especially mothers, with more education provide better nutrition to their children, have healthier children, are less fertile, and are more concerned that their children be educated. Education—in particular, female education—is key to reducing poverty and must be considered as much a part of a country's health strategy as, say, programs of immunization and access to health clinics.

Education is thus more important for economic development and poverty reduction than it used to be or was understood to be. It deserves a higher priority

TABLE 5.1   RATES OF RETURN TO INVESTMENTS IN DIFFERENT SECTORS OF THE ECONOMY

Item	1974–82	1983–92	1974–92
Education investments			
Primary			20
Secondary			14
Higher			11
World Bank projects			
Agriculture	14	11	
Industry	15	12	
Infrastructure	18	16	
All projects	17	15	

Sources: Psacharopoulos 1994; World Bank 1994n; World Bank Operations Evaluation Department database.

from governments as a whole—not only from ministries of education but also from ministries of finance and planning. The need for such an emphasis has long been realized by countries in East Asia and is increasingly coming to be understood in other areas, especially in Latin America and India. It is important that education receive more attention elsewhere, too, especially in Africa, South Asia, the Middle East, and the former socialist countries of Europe and Asia, most of which have until recently been appropriately preoccupied with shorter-term issues of economic reform. The return to a longer-term focus on development and poverty reduction implies a higher priority for education, with specific policies and priorities within education varying according to country circumstances. At the same time, too much must not be claimed for education. Its contribution to the reduction of poverty depends critically on complementary macroeconomic policies and investments in physical assets.

CHAPTER SIX

Attention to Outcomes

AN ORIENTATION toward outcomes means that priorities in education are determined through economic analysis, standard setting, and measurement of the attainment of standards. A sectoral approach is key for setting priorities. While governments determine priorities for many reasons, economic analysis of education—in particular, rate of return analysis—is a diagnostic tool with which to start the process of setting priorities and considering alternative ways of achieving objectives within a sectoral approach. The reasons for determining priorities vary country by country and even government by government, and this report's call for more attention to the impact of educational outcomes does not suggest that these other reasons are inappropriate. Rather, it argues that insufficient attention is generally given to outcomes, whether defined in labor market or in learning terms.

Using Outcomes to Set and Monitor Public Priorities

Most governments typically define how much education should be available for everyone implicitly, through legislation regarding the school starting age, compulsory school attendance laws, regulations on the minimum work age, constitutional stipulations, and nationally ratified international conventions. Countries fall short of their goals (table 6.1) largely because they do not allocate sufficient resources to achieve them. Even where resources are available,

TABLE 6.1 COMPULSORY EDUCATION, ENROLLMENT RATIOS AND MINIMUM AGE
FOR EMPLOYMENT, SELECTED COUNTRIES, 1990S

Country	Compulsory education (duration in years)	Primary gross enrollment ratio, 1990 (percent)			Minimum age for employment (1992)
		Total	Male	Female	
Bangladesh	5	77	83	71	12
Côte d'Ivoire	6	69	81	58	14
El Salvador	9	79	78	79	14
Guatemala	6	79	84	74	14
Guinea-Bissau	6	60	77	42	14
Malawi	8	66	73	60	14
Morocco	9	65	77	53	12
Senegal	6	58	68	49	14

Sources: ILO 1992; UNESCO 1993b.

however, the emphasis solely on years in school is misplaced. More appropriate would be an emphasis on knowledge and skills. School attendance is a means, not an end; it contributes to the acquisition of skills, knowledge, and attitudes. It is what students learn that is important.

Basic education is the top priority in all countries because it provides the basic skills and knowledge necessary for civic order and full participation in society, as well as for all forms of work. The skills and knowledge acquired at the upper-secondary and tertiary levels, by contrast, are applied more explicitly in the labor market, and economic analysis can help to guide public sector investments at these levels.

Economic analysis applied to education focuses on the assessment of benefits and costs, for individuals and for society as a whole. The costs of alternative interventions to achieve a given educational objective are compared, and the relationship between benefits and costs is measured—usually, by calculating the rate of return, taking as the benefit enhanced labor productivity as measured by differential wages (see box 1.1). Both the social rate of return and the difference between the social and private rates of return can help in setting public sector priorities. The priorities for public investment determined by this type of economic analysis are those in which the social rate of return is highest and the level of public subsidization is lowest.

The contrast between the social and private rates of return to investment in education, using wage differentials as the benefit measure, highlights the extent of public subsidization of education (see table 1.1). An index of public subsidization (the percentage by which the private rate exceeds the social rate) can be calculated. In most countries higher education is the most heavily subsidized level of education. In Paraguay, for example, the private and social rates of return to primary education are 23.7 and 20.3 percent, respectively, while the private and social returns to higher education are 13.7 and 10.8 percent. The index of public subsidization in this case is 27 percent for higher education and only 17 percent for primary education (Psacharopoulos, Velez, and Patrinos 1994).

These rates of return must be calculated in specific country circumstances and cannot be assumed. Methodological considerations and the practical problems associated with the valuation of external benefits mean that it is prudent to exercise caution and use good judgment when applying cost-benefit analysis. For instance, rates of return are normally based on current average earnings differentials, which are known to remain stable over long periods of time. Where possible, however, earnings differentials at the margin should be used for workers in sectors with free entry. Estimates of rates of return are also slow to reflect new developments in the labor market, such as growing imbalances between employers' demand and the output of the education system.

Aside from these difficulties, the calculation of private rates of return to education is relatively straightforward. That of the social rates is more problematic. No consensus exists on how to quantify and evaluate the social externalities of education. The common practice is therefore simply to calculate social returns by adjusting private returns downward to allow for the public sector's net expenditures on education and to ignore potential offsetting external benefits. Again, judgment must be used; the cost-benefit framework of economic analysis provides a key diagnostic tool that points policymakers in certain directions, rather than a precision indicator for setting priorities.

Once priorities have been set and financing arrangements put in place, it is necessary to pay close attention to the costs of educational investments and to attempt to reduce unit costs by improving efficiency. Cost-effectiveness analysis that compares alternative ways of achieving the same result is needed. The most cost-effective technique is the one that produces the desired result at minimum cost or yields the largest gain in educational achievement for a given cost. For example, cost-effectiveness analysis has shown that laboratories are not necessary for acquiring basic scientific competency. It has also been used to assess the cost of instructing students at a consolidated school or at multiple schools.

Basic education provides the essential knowledge, skills, and attitudes for functioning effectively in society. Basic competencies in such general areas as verbal, computational, communication, and problem-solving skills can be applied in a wide range of work settings and can enable people to acquire job-specific skills and knowledge in the workplace (Becker 1964). This basic level typically requires about eight years of schooling.

Basic skills are increasingly important in all societies. In the United States between 1978 and 1986 the wage premium associated with mastery of elementary mathematics rose from $0.46 to $1.15 per hour for men and from $1.15 to $1.42 for women, for people with the same number of years of schooling (Murnane, Willet, and Levy 1993). East Africans with good basic skills are more likely to enter the modern wage labor market and to earn higher wages than are less literate and less numerate workers with the same number of years of schooling. Secondary-school leavers who scored in the top third on the school-leaving examination earn 50 percent more than those in the bottom third in Kenya and about 35 percent more in Tanzania (Boissière, Knight, and Sabot 1985).

The high rates of return estimated for basic education in most developing countries strongly suggest that investments to expand enrollments and improve retention in basic education should generally be the highest-priority education investments in countries which have not yet achieved universal basic education. In many cases, expanded basic education coverage will require investments to expand school capacity, to train qualified teachers, and to provide suitable educational materials. But in other cases, where insufficient capacity is not the binding constraint, the demand for education will need to be increased through actions designed to improve educational quality, to improve the school environment, or to defray the direct and indirect costs of school attendance. This is particularly so in poor settings where children contribute more to the household than they consume (Lindert 1976).

Other education interventions may also merit a high priority. Investments to improve educational quality or efficiency often have high rates of return. In some cases these returns may be even higher than for investments to expand education coverage. The benefits of investments to improve efficiency in education—for example, through improved student retention or more intensive use of staff and facilities—can typically be expressed in terms of reduced unit costs per student or per graduate. Although the benefits of improved educational quality—for example, as indicated by prospective earnings—are more difficult to measure, they should nonetheless be weighed explicitly in considering the relative priority of such investments.

In addition to these investments, some improvements in educational efficiency or quality will often be possible through policy changes requiring no specific investments. For example, more efficient assignment of existing teachers could reduce the need for recruitment of new teachers in some education systems.

Decisions about priorities for public spending on education beyond the basic level have to be taken within a broad sectoral approach. A distinction needs to be made between countries that have achieved, or almost achieved, universal basic education and those that have not. Countries that have achieved universal basic education are likely to consider upper-secondary and higher education the priorities for new public spending.

Decisions about public priorities among these postcompulsory levels can be informed by the prudent use of economic analysis focusing on labor market outcomes and other social benefits. Economic analysis has shown, for example, that the average social rates of return to general secondary education are much higher than those to highly specialized vocational secondary education (Psacharopoulos 1987, 1994). This result is consistent with the constant and rapid changes in technology and labor markets that call for flexible, "trainable" workers able to acquire new skills as technology changes. The preferable way to achieve this goal is to emphasize learning skills and attitudes rather than specific job-related skills that are best taught in specific job settings. For example, in Indonesia, a rapidly industrializing country, the returns to academic and vocational secondary education fell between 1979 and 1986, but returns to academic secondary education nevertheless remained higher (11 percent, down from 32 percent) than those to vocational secondary education (9 percent, down from 18 percent).

The low returns to secondary vocational education signal that additional investment under current conditions would be inefficient. Reducing the provision of places is, however, not necessarily the correct policy response. For vocational education, the low returns could be attributable to high costs rather than to a lack of demand for technically skilled labor. Therefore, one alternative would be to reduce costs in order to raise the returns. Possible reforms would include shortening the duration of the course and reducing unit operating costs. If the returns do not increase significantly, alternative arrangements for training skilled workers outside the formal school system might be appropriate (Mingat and Tan 1985).

Complementary tools for assessing investment priorities include tracer studies and annual routines (Mingat and Tan 1985; Sapsford and Tzannatos 1993). These can be used to collect data relating to school programs and to monitor labor market trends affecting recent school leavers. This type of information should be collected annually, as it provides useful feedback on the effects of recent policies so that adjustments can be made to the system. The annual routine can improve the responsiveness of investment decisions to new labor market conditions. It increases the external efficiency of educational investments within the broad strategies suggested by the rate of return analysis.

The advantage of economic analysis is that assumptions must be stated at the outset. In the above example, it is assumed that there is a demand for the output of the secondary vocational stream. But empirical analysis can be used to check this assumption. One direct method is through employer surveys, as in Indonesia. There, the results show an inconsistency between the public and private perceptions of the skills development problem; private companies do not view skill shortages as a problem, and most companies provide their own training (Dhanani 1993).

Estimates of rates of return to investments in education are not very relevant when the labor market is not competitive—or does not exist, as was the case in the socialist economies of Eastern Europe. The dramatic economic changes in these countries are expected to result in a premium on entrepreneurial ability as workers for the first time face a competitive labor market where success is rewarded. As Nobel laureate T. W. Schultz has argued, entrepreneurial ability complements education and work experience. Therefore, relative returns to education should rise in the newly emerging market economies in comparison with returns before the transition, when entrepreneurial skills were not needed.

Empirical analysis of changes in the wage structure in Slovenia between 1987 and 1991 reveals that the returns to human capital (as measured, in this case, by years of schooling) rise dramatically during transitions (Orazem and Vodopivec 1994). In comparisons of educated and least-educated groups, those with four years of university education gained the most in relative earnings, followed by those with two years of university; those with vocational qualifications gained least. Major changes in the economy—transition to a market economy, restructuring, trade liberalization, and new economic alliances such as the North American Free Trade Agreement—should therefore result in greater gains to those with more education and a more general education.

Vocational education in high-income countries and in some upper-middle-income countries is accordingly becoming less specialized; it now typically includes a very extensive general education component. At the same time, general secondary education now typically also includes technology education, designed to facilitate entry into the world of work. Also increasingly common are school-to-work programs that combine general education at school with one or two days per week of work on the job and so accustom students to the attitudes required at work. This convergence of vocational and general secondary education and the linkage of school and work in OECD countries has yet to be evaluated using economic analysis, but it seems likely to yield higher returns than narrow vocational education.

Many low- and middle-income countries with universal primary and lower secondary education now have large, highly specialized upper-secondary vocational programs. In the former command economies of Eastern and Central Europe, the bulk of upper-secondary schooling consists of extremely specialized vocational and technical education. In Poland, for instance, only 20 percent of secondary students are in general education, even though the emerging market economy requires workers with a general education (World Bank 1992). Labor markets themselves are only now emerging in Eastern Europe and Central Asia, and the relationship between them and the education system has still to develop.

Countries cannot quickly reduce the size of such large vocational secondary programs, but the programs should increasingly be made more general and linked to the development of attitudes and general skills, rather than specific skills, necessary for work. Evidence on labor market outcomes indicates that, over time, reducing the vocational share of secondary education is advisable.

There are countries in which the returns to some types of specialized vocational education have been found at some times to be higher than those to general secondary education. This finding reflects shortages of certain skills in the labor market. In Chile, for example, the returns to agricultural training, industrial skills, and commercial skills are all currently higher than those to general secondary education. Hence the central government subsidizes municipally run vocational centers, with the amount of the subsidy varying according to labor market needs. In 1993 agricultural schools received 200 percent of the subsidy to general secondary schools, industrial schools 150 percent, and commercial schools 125 percent (Cox-Edwards 1994).

Countries that have yet to achieve near-universal basic education face simpler decisions in determining priorities. Given the importance of achieving full coverage of basic education, economic analysis can help guide public choice about investments above these levels to select those that will clearly have a greater impact on labor productivity and other social benefits. In most countries the priority for new investment will clearly be basic education, but science at the upper-secondary level and science and engineering at the higher level may be exceptions. If the social rate of return to these courses, or to specialized vocational courses, is higher than that to primary and lower-secondary education, there will be a case for increased public investment. So far, few economic analyses have included this degree of specificity, but governments can use such analyses in specific country circumstances to guide investment decisions (McMahon and Jung 1989).

Setting Standards and Monitoring Performance

Once the public sector has made decisions concerning allocation of public resources, an important step is to define the skills and competencies to be acquired at each level of publicly financed education and to monitor their acquisition. There is much scope for broader use of mechanisms for setting standards and monitoring learning outcomes (see chapter 4) and, ideally, for more use of internationally agreed definitions. The OECD, for instance, is proposing the continuous monitoring of three categories of standard outcome indicators for its member countries: student outcomes, system outcomes, and labor market outcomes. Student outcomes include performance in reading, mathematics, and science and gender differences in reading achievement; system outcomes include upper-secondary graduation, university graduation, science and engineering degrees, and science and engineering personnel. Labor market outcomes include unemployment, education, and earnings (Tuijnman and Postlethwaite 1994).

After standards for performance have been established, performance needs to be observed and linked to incentives. A variety of performance indicators can be used, including, but not limited to, tests and examinations. What is tested tends to be what is taught, and public examinations, in particular, have considerable potential for improving the quality of student learning (Kellaghan and Greaney 1992). But serious problems can arise if (a) examinations are linked to instruction in such a way that the curriculum is narrowed, (b) an emphasis is placed on examination techniques and rote-memorized knowledge; and (c) past examinations start to dictate not only what is taught but how it is taught. Public examinations to raise quality cannot be the same as those for selection, as the latter do not take account of the needs of the majority of students who are not proceeding to the next level.

Performance measures have both policy and pedagogical applications. They can be used to monitor progress toward national educational goals, evaluate the effectiveness and efficiency of specific policies and programs, hold schools accountable for performance of students, select and certify students, and provide feedback to teachers about individual students' learning needs (Larach and Lockheed 1992). They can also be linked with incentives to drive a system toward higher achievement.

Internationally, there is greater experience with the use of performance indicators for individual accountability than for institutional accountability. Examinations for selection and certification, often but not always linked to the curriculum, are found worldwide (Eckstein and Noah 1993). As a pedagogical practice, teachers typically use tests and quizzes to monitor student learning.

The use of performance measures for institutional accountability is still fairly recent. Experience so far shows that such practice has potential, but also that this potential is limited. Holding schools fully accountable for their students' performance can be difficult because (a) statistically valid distinctions among schools cannot always be made; (b) comparisons of schools may not correct for differences in student intakes, in terms of socioeconomic status, or the social and physical conditions under which the schools operate; (c) school rankings can vary according to the particular outcome measure that is used; and

(d) as an outcome of the publication of results, schools that are perceived to be doing well may attract students of high ability, to the detriment of schools that are perceived to be doing badly but may in fact be doing well for their intake and conditions (Greaney and Kellaghan 1995).

More recently, performance measures have been used to target resources and have been linked to incentives for improvement. In Chile results from a national assessment system in four subjects have been combined with other social indicators to assist the Ministry of Education in targeting additional support to the poorest schools (Himmel 1995). Each potential recipient school is reviewed according to the average student performance on the SIMCE (the national assessment test), the school's socioeconomic level, rural-urban location, and number of primary grades offered; the test score counts as 50 percent of the school score. On the basis of the score, the schools are rated as "high," "medium," or "low" risk; 46 percent of the available resources for school improvement are targeted to high-risk schools and another 46 percent to medium-risk schools. Within risk categories, schools compete for funds by proposing school improvement activities to be supported. In 1995 school-level scores on SIMCE will provide evidence regarding the effectiveness of four different educational interventions to be tested on a pilot basis before widespread introduction; interventions that do not boost learning will not be eligible for larger-scale implementation. Particularly important is the inclusion of socioeconomic status. Similarly, in New Zealand schools are funded in part in reverse proportion to the socioeconomic status of their students' families. Such mechanisms ensure both incentives for higher achievement and the provision of resources to needier schools.

In many countries national learning assessment systems are enabling ministries of education to monitor their own progress, evaluate the potential impact and cost-effectiveness of experimental programs, and improve the quality of their educational planning. Information from national assessments can inform teaching and learning processes when this information is disseminated broadly. The World Bank and other donors are assisting many countries to strengthen the institutions responsible for national public examination and assessment systems (Larach and Lockheed 1992). This strengthened capacity will enable donors to monitor the effect of their support on an important development goal—the learning achievement of children. Networking among countries that are introducing learning assessments is also an increasingly important factor in improving their implementation.

The World Bank is encouraging the use of performance and effectiveness indicators in the education projects that it helps finance. Especially important here are labor market and learning outcomes and the relationship of outcomes to inputs.

CHAPTER SEVEN

Public Investment Focused on Basic Education

GOVERNMENTS invest in education for many reasons. This chapter looks at public investment in education from the strictly economic viewpoint of maximizing both efficiency and equity. In practice, other objectives are always present in decisions about public investment, but more attention to efficiency and equity in the allocation of new public investment on education would do much to meet the challenges that education systems face today. Such attention would lead to new public investment being focused on basic education in most countries. (This emphasis will clearly be least applicable to those countries that already have achieved near-universal enrollment ratios in basic education.)

To achieve efficiency, public resources should be concentrated in a cost-effective manner where the returns to investment are highest. To achieve equity, the government needs to ensure that no qualified student is denied access to education because of inability to pay. At the same time, and because the gap between the private and social returns is larger for higher education than for basic education, advantage should be taken of any willingness to pay for higher education by sharing its costs with students and their parents. Governments can also intervene. By bearing some of the risk, they can help correct the capital market failures that preclude financial institutions from lending for higher education.

Combining these principles would result in a policy package of fees and efficient expenditure in the public sector. The elements of this package—which would have to be adapted to particular circumstances—would usually be:

■ Free public basic education, combined with targeted stipends for households that cannot afford to enroll their children and with cost-sharing with communities.

■ Selective charging of fees for upper-secondary education, again combined with targeted scholarships.

■ Fees for all public higher education, combined with loan, tax and other schemes so that students who cannot afford to pay the fees out of their own or their parents' current income may defer payment until they have income themselves. This fee system would be accompanied by a targeted scholarship scheme to overcome the reluctance of the poor to accumulate debt against future earnings of which they are not yet confident.

■ A goal of quality primary education for all children as the priority for public spending on education in all countries.

■ Improvement of access to quality general secondary education (initially lower-secondary and later all levels of secondary) over time.

■ Efficient spending at the school and institution levels in the public sector.

Korea is an example of a country that follows most of these policies. Fees (including Parent-Teacher Association dues) account for only 2 percent of recurrent costs at the primary level but for 41 percent at the middle school level, 73 percent at the high school level, and 77 percent at the tertiary level. Overall, the private costs of education account for about 50 percent of recurrent costs for the entire education system (Adams and Gottlieb 1993). Public expenditure is heavily concentrated on basic education: 44 percent for primary education, 34 percent for middle and high school education, and 7 percent for higher education.

Pricing Policy for Public Education

Basic Education

A complete basic education is normally provided free of fees, since it is essential for the acquisition of the knowledge, skills, and attitudes needed by society. The definition of basic education is country-specific, but it typically encompasses at least primary education and often lower-secondary education, as well (although not always, as the example of Korea shows). The importance of primary education, in particular, is confirmed when externalities are taken into account. To obtain the maximum gain for society as a whole, the top public priority is the acquisition of basic competencies by all students. Achievement of this goal requires increasing demand and ensuring access for every child through free basic education. Indonesia, Kenya, and Tanzania increased their enrollments significantly after abolishing primary school fees (Colletta and Sutton 1989; Lockheed, Verspoor, and others 1991). Côte d'Ivoire made the mistake of introducing fees when the demand for primary schooling was already declining. Unofficial fees and charges can be a barrier to enrollments in primary education, as in Ghana in 1992, when first-year intakes fell by more than 4 percent. Public schools should not, of course, be prohibited from mobilizing resources, in cash or in kind, from local communities when public financing is inadequate and such extra resources constitute the only means of achieving quality.

Even when public basic education is free, there will be poor households that cannot afford to send their children to school or keep them in school because of direct and indirect costs, such as buying books or losing production around the home. Targeted stipends can help these households offset the income lost when children attend school. Such a scheme, for girls, operates in thirteen Guatemalan communities. Thailand provides bicycles to students in rural areas to enable them to reach distant schools (Lockheed, Verspoor, and others 1991). Many World Bank projects have financed free textbooks and uniforms for poor families, and a few have included experiments with direct stipends at the secondary level.

Cost-sharing with communities is normally the only exception to free basic education. Even very poor communities are often willing to contribute toward the cost of education, especially at the primary level. In Nepal, for example, almost all primary and many secondary schools are built and maintained by local communities. Matching-grant schemes may increase local involvement in schools, create a sense of ownership, and encourage greater private contributions to education. Such schemes are increasingly common in Africa and in Latin America. Brazil, Ghana, India, and Tanzania are experimenting with matching-grant schemes for school construction, with World Bank support. In Brazil public funding is conditional on local communities achieving agreed targets for contributions of materials and labor for school construction.

Many countries, including Bolivia, Cameroon, Ethiopia, Honduras, Senegal, Uganda, and Zambia, have set up social investment funds. These programs induce community participation, investment in employment generation, and provision of basic social services. World Bank projects support such funds in twenty-two countries. In Ghana the government contributes up to two-thirds of the total project cost, and the communities supply labor and local materials. This approach has cut the construction time for new schools to about three months (World Bank 1991a). Through tripartite arrangements the World Bank–supported Social Rehabilitation Fund in Ethiopia finances building materials and school equipment, the community contributes labor, and the Ministry of Education provides a teacher. All these contributions are included in formal contracts.

Upper-Secondary Education

Since upper-secondary-school graduates will have higher earnings than those who leave school earlier, selectively charging fees for public secondary school can help to increase enrollments. Cost-sharing with communities can be encouraged at the secondary, as well as the primary, level. Fees can be usually charged without affecting overall enrollments, but enrollments of the poor and of girls do fall unless offsetting measures are taken. There is considerable evidence that household demand for education is relatively price-inelastic— that is, unresponsive to increases in private costs (Jimenez 1987; World Bank 1986), except among the very poor. Indeed, inelasticity of demand could be a useful criterion for making decisions about charging fees. In Peru household survey data show that a moderate increase in fees does not affect the overall demand for secondary education, although it does discourage enrollments by the lowest income groups (Gertler and Glewwe 1989). Poorer families have difficulty meeting the direct and indirect costs of children's school attendance. To offset this hardship, secondary school fees can be combined with targeted scholarships and stipends to ensure equity in enrollments. If scholarships equivalent to fees and the direct costs of schooling were provided to the poorest 20 percent of Indonesian households, for instance, dropout rates at lower-secondary schools could be cut in half (World Bank 1993c). The Bank has supported such targeted scholarship schemes for girls in Bangladesh and Pakistan and for poor families in Colombia.

The charging of fees at one level can affect enrollments by other family members at other levels. A poor family that has to pay fees for an upper-secondary student may not be able to enroll other children in primary school because the younger children's work is needed to generate the income from which the fees are to be paid (Chernichovsky 1985). This dilemma is precisely why fee charging must be accompanied by targeted stipends to enable the enrollment of students from poor families. Fees used without compensatory measures will have a negative impact on the enrollment of such children.

Higher Education

In general, fees are justified at public institutions for higher education. Also acceptable is the elimination of subsidies for such noninstructional costs as student housing and meals, except where income taxation systems are very progressive or include a graduate tax (Colclough 1990); either measure can permit recovery of the costs of higher education from lifetime earnings. Most developing countries have neither an effective nor a progressive income tax, however, and a graduate tax or a system of fees and loans would be a more equitable way of recovering costs. Few countries have tried to use graduate taxes.

As with upper-secondary students, the demand for higher education is relatively price-inelastic. A 10 percent increase in fees in Thailand would result in only a 2 percent drop in enrollment (Chutikul 1986). An optimal policy would be full cost recovery by public higher education institutions, with students paying fees out of parental income and out of their own future incomes, through a loan scheme or a graduate tax. Such a policy is very distant in all countries, however, because fee levels are so low and experience with loan schemes has been relatively disappointing.

A good start in the right direction would be to charge fees covering 100 percent of the recurrent cost of student welfare services, such as food and housing, and 30 percent of instructional costs. Several countries, including Chile, Jamaica, and Korea, are well on their way toward this target (table 7.1). Others have very far to go. In Senegal welfare payments to tertiary students accounted for nearly half of total public spending on higher education in the mid-1980s. In the Sahel countries of West Africa, welfare services account for 57 percent of public spending on higher education, compared with 7 percent in Asia (table 7.2). Malaysia, by contrast, has contracted out student food services to private suppliers who recover all costs, and it is discussing privatization of student housing.

Student loan schemes are an essential complement to cost recovery and the charging of fees. Many students are unable to afford the cost of higher education out of their families' current income, and loan schemes permit them to pay out of their future earnings. About fifty countries, industrial and developing, have such schemes. More than half are in Latin America; other developing countries with loan schemes include China, Ghana, Egypt, India, Jordan, Kenya, Korea, Malawi, Malaysia, Morocco, Pakistan, the Philippines, and Sri Lanka.

In most countries loans are repaid according to a fixed schedule; in a few, including Australia, Ghana, and Sweden, they are repaid as a proportion of a

TABLE 7.1 FEES FOR PUBLIC HIGHER EDUCATION AS A SHARE OF UNIT OPERATING EXPENDITURE, SELECTED COUNTRIES

Country and year of data	Percent	Country and year of data	Percent
Algeria, 1990	0	Bolivia, 1991	3
Argentina, 1990	0	Honduras, 1991	3
Bangladesh, mid-1980s	0	Sri Lanka, mid-1980s	3
Benin, 1991	0	Egypt, 1990	4
Brazil, 1991	0	Pakistan, 1990	4
Ghana, 1990	0	India, mid-1980s	5
Guinea, 1990	0	Thailand, mid-1980s	5
Madagascar, 1990	0	Malaysia, mid-1980s	6
Malawi, 1990	0	China, 1991	9
Mexico, 1991	0	Japan, 1991	9
Morocco, 1990	0	Colombia, 1991	10
Niger, 1991	0	Nepal, mid-1980s	10
Nigeria, 1989	0	Kenya, 1991	12
Papua New Guinea, mid-1980s	0	Barbados, 1991	15
Peru, 1991	0	Philippines, mid-1980s	15
Senegal, 1990	0	United States, 1985	15
Sudan, 1987	0	Costa Rica, 1991	16
Uganda, 1991	0	Israel, 1991	20
United Kingdom, 1990	0	Spain, 1988	20
Venezuela, 1991	0	Korea, Rep. of, mid-1980s	23
France, 1990	1	Viet Nam, 1991	23
Guatemala, 1991	2	Indonesia, 1989	25
Hungary, 1990	2	Jamaica, 1991	25
		Chile, 1991	26

Note: Expenditures on student housing are excluded.
Source: Ziderman and Albrecht 1995.

graduate's income each year. Experience to date has been relatively disappointing. Heavily subsidized interest rates, high default rates, and high administrative costs have led to very low recovery ratios (Albrecht and Ziderman 1991). Losses range from 30 percent in Sweden to 103 percent in Kenya, where the interest rate is heavily subsidized, administrative costs are high, and very few graduates repay their loans. In large part, the reason for this anemic performance is that loan schemes have been administered by government ministries and agencies rather than by financial institutions such as banks.

TABLE 7.2 SHARE OF SECONDARY AND HIGHER EDUCATION BUDGET DEVOTED TO STUDENT WELFARE, SUB-SAHARAN AFRICA AND ASIA, ABOUT 1985

Country	Secondary	Tertiary
Sahelian countries	18.1	56.5
Burkina Faso	35.0	79.0
Chad	0.0	32.9
Mali	19.0	66.8
Mauritania	18.6	56.9
Niger	22.7	59.5
Senegal	13.2	43.9
Non-Sahelian Sub-Saharan Africa		
French speaking	24.9	57.0
English speaking	7.5	23.2
Asia	5.1	7.2

Source: Jarousse and Mingat 1993.

Loan schemes can be made financially sustainable, as the experiences of Quebec (Canada) and Colombia demonstrate. They require that the public sector bear some of the risk, since banks and other financial institutions are generally unwilling to accept students' likely future earnings as collateral. Public sector intervention is appropriate to offset this failure of the capital market. The World Bank is supporting loan-scheme reform in Jamaica, Kenya, Malawi, the Philippines, Tunisia, and Venezuela. Sustainable loan schemes require an effective collection agency with incentives to minimize evasion and default. Interest rates must be positive in real terms. Income-contingent and graduated annual payment schemes are needed to encourage repayment commensurate with the student's future earnings, which will rise over time.

Loan schemes alone will not suffice to enroll low-income students in higher education. Even though their future earnings will be high, students from poor backgrounds are understandably reluctant to take on debt against future earnings that may not seem certain to them. In addition, while pursuing higher education, they forgo earnings that may be important for their families' income. Targeted scholarships and work-study programs are needed to overcome this problem. Work-study, in particular, can help low-income students finance their living costs, if not their tuition. In most countries students come from relatively well-off backgrounds and have high earnings prospects, and so the bulk of financial assistance should be provided through loans rather than scholarships.

Two alternatives to loan schemes are graduate taxes and national service. Graduate taxes are supplementary income tax payments made by university graduates. It is difficult to assess the potential of such tax schemes because no country has yet adopted one. In national service schemes students receive subsidies to attend higher education institutions and then work for society at below-market salaries. Nepal and Nigeria have had successful programs in which graduates went on to provide social services in rural areas. Several other countries, including the United States, are considering introducing such programs. National service schemes can run the danger of turning into schemes of guaranteed public employment for higher education graduates.

Priorities for Public Spending

Basic education is the priority for public policy and hence also for public expenditure in all countries. The objective is usually to have all children enroll in and complete primary and, ultimately, lower-secondary school and to learn effectively in school so that they acquire basic skills. This goal is consistent with the objective adopted in 1990 by the World Conference on Education for All and supported by the World Bank. It is both efficient and equitable, having the highest returns and increasing educational and earnings opportunities for the whole population (World Bank 1990a). To achieve high enrollments and sustained performance, expenditure at the primary level may also need to be complemented by targeted expenditure on early childhood development for poor families.

As primary enrollment ratios go up, increasing public resources will be devoted to secondary education. Demographic change, in part fueled by primary education for girls, can help this process. For example, Korea has been able to increase public secondary enrollments and increase spending per student at both primary and secondary levels without increasing the share of national income devoted to public spending on education. By the late 1980s lowered fertility rates allowed East Asian countries to spend a significantly lower share of GNP on primary and secondary education, compared with countries with higher fertility rates (table 7.3).

Countries that have largely achieved universal primary and secondary education face different challenges in determining priorities for public spending on education. Higher education will take on a greater relative priority for public expenditure, as it does in OECD countries. It is important, however, that attention to higher education not deflect spending from the basic levels, where

TABLE 7.3   SAVINGS IN GNP ALLOCATED TO EDUCATION AS A RESULT OF LOWER
FERTILITY RATES IN EAST ASIA

Economy	Expenditure on primary and secondary education as a percentage of GNP	Percentage of GNP saved due to growth rates of school-age population that were lower than those in:		
		Kenya	Mexico	Pakistan
Hong Kong				
1975	2.0	1.2	1.0	1.0
1980–81	1.7	1.5	1.7	1.2
Japan				
1975	4.2	4.0	3.8	3.8
1988–89	2.8	4.8	2.8	3.9
Korea, Rep. of				
1975	1.9	0.6	0.4	0.4
1988–89	2.8	2.8	1.4	2.0
Malaysia				
1980–81	4.4	1.3	0.4	0.4
1988–89	4.0	1.6	0.4	0.8
Singapore				
1975	2.1	1.1	0.8	2.0
1980–81	2.2	2.0	1.3	1.3
Thailand				
1975	2.8	0.6	0.0	0.0
1988–89	2.6	1.3	0.3	0.8

Source: World Bank 1993a, table 5.2.

quality remains relatively low in low- and middle-income countries and where
economic restructuring threatens the maintenance of adequate funding. In Russia, for instance, it is important to ensure that compulsory education remains
adequately funded as financing responsibility shifts from the federal level to
the state governments. It is also important to ensure that essential preschool
programs, previously provided by public enterprises, be funded, at least for
poor children, as the enterprises withdraw from this responsibility.

Sustainability

A particularly important issue in the public financing of education is fiscal sustainability. To achieve this, policies are needed to increase the efficiency of public spending, to increase public spending when appropriate, and to complement public with private financing (chapter 3). To ensure sustainability, it is always advisable to project the fiscal impact of expenditure measures several years into the future and to have sound financing plans.

CHAPTER EIGHT

Attention to Equity

ACHIEVING equity—an important goal for many governments—often requires more attention than it has received in the past. This is particularly true at the first level of schooling, especially when systems include private schools and private financing.

The government has two fundamental concerns regarding equity. The first is to ensure that everyone has a basic education—the basic competencies necessary to function effectively in society. The second is to ensure that qualified potential students are not denied access to institutions because they are poor or female, are from ethnic minorities, live in geographically remote regions, or have special education needs. No qualified student should be unable to enroll because of inability to pay. To determine who is qualified at the postcompulsory level, a fair and valid means for assessing potential students' qualifications for entry is needed.

Increased attention to equity will also increase efficiency. Considerable evidence now exists that improving the educational status of the poor, of women, and of indigenous people increases economic growth and reduces poverty. Investing in the education of girls from poor backgrounds sets off a process of intergenerational poverty reduction: educated women are more likely to send their own children to school. The well-known efficiency arguments for improving girls' schooling (Summers 1994) apply also to indigenous people. Had Guatemala invested in education to raise secondary enrollment ratios from 7 to

50 percent in 1960, for example, the country's per capita growth rate during 1960-85 would probably have been higher by 1.3 percentage points per year (Gould and Ruffin 1993; Barro 1991).

Achieving equity at the first level of schooling is a matter of both increasing the demand for education and meeting that demand through financing and special measures. Financing is important at all levels for those who cannot afford to go to school—either because they and their parents cannot pay the associated costs or because the household cannot afford to lose their labor services. Special measures tend to be concentrated on the lower levels of education. They include recruiting more female teachers to provide role models for girls, making special education available, providing bilingual education in countries with linguistic diversity, and conducting health and nutrition programs. Taken together, these measures amount to providing universal access to learning (not just universal school attendance) at the primary level, which opens the way to equity at all levels of the education system.

Financial Measures

In most countries public primary education is free; lower-secondary education is often free as well. Even when there is no tuition charge, however, the direct and indirect costs for poor families can be too high to ensure enrollment and learning. Direct costs can include transport, textbooks, exercise books, pencils, uniforms, and the like. If poor children lack these items, they may not attend school or may not learn. In Kenya during the 1980s the government made parents responsible for providing books. By 1990 in the poor arid and semiarid areas there was frequently only one book per class. The policy was reversed in 1992 for the poor areas of the country, with the support of a World Bank adjustment operation. In Morocco parents' reluctance to send daughters to school without proper clothing increases the direct cost of sending girls to school compared with boys. Funding assistance is also needed for the poor when the indirect costs of attending school are high in comparison with the child's contribution to the household economy. It is often more difficult for parents to send a girl to school than a boy because girls contribute more hours of work at home than do boys. In Burkina Faso girls age 7 and over spend 3.5 hours a day on household tasks, compared with 1.5 hours for boys (Chowdhury 1993).

The use of child labor reduces the demand for schooling, again because of poor families' need for income. Children work for a variety of reasons, the most important being poverty and the pressure to escape from it. Although children are not well paid, they still make major contributions to family income in developing countries. For example, minors in Paraguay contribute almost a

BOX 8.1   REDUCING THE HOUSEHOLD
COSTS OF GIRLS' EDUCATION
IN BANGLADESH

In Bangladesh the World Bank–supported Female Secondary School Assistance Project provides stipends to girls. The stipend rates are structured to reflect rising educational costs from lower to upper grades and to provide extra incentives for reducing high dropout rates in upper grades. Students must maintain a certain grade average to continue to earn stipends.

The project also supports a number of other measures to encourage female school enrollment. These include increasing the proportion of women teachers and conducting a community awareness program to promote public support for girls' education.

quarter of total family income (Patrinos and Psacharopoulos 1995). In rural Java, Indonesia, a typical 13-year-old boy from a poor household earns about $11 a month as an agricultural laborer, contributing, on average, about 40 percent to the household income. This income is more than twice the average per student direct expenditure on lower-secondary education among poor households (Mason 1994). These figures are underestimates, since they do not include the value of children's contributions to home production.

One reason why parents' demand for educating daughters is low is the associated direct and opportunity costs in many countries, including Bangladesh, Egypt, Guatemala, Mali, Morocco, Peru, Tunisia, and Yemen. Some projects have cut these costs by waiving or reducing fees, supplying free textbooks, providing scholarships or stipends for girls, offering flexible school hours, and establishing childcare centers. Such approaches, in addition to reducing costs to parents, improve school quality, reduce dropout rates, improve the efficiency of the school system, and significantly increase girls' effective participation. Bangladesh and Guatemala have girls' scholarship programs in which tuition is free and stipends are paid to parents to compensate them for other direct costs, such as books, and for the loss of their daughters' time. Bank-supported projects provide stipends for girls at secondary school in Bangladesh (box 8.1), scholarships for rural girls in Morocco and Mozambique, and incentives for girls in the Gambia to study science. More analysis is needed of the effect of these schemes on school quality and of their fiscal sustainability.

Targeted scholarship schemes can be used to increase the demand for education among all disadvantaged groups, not just women. Several middle-income countries are experimenting with targeted scholarship schemes for students who cannot afford fees. These schemes cover the cost of tuition but do not provide any compensation to the family for the loss of the child's time. The targeted vouchers used in Colombia and in the U.S. commonwealth of Puerto Rico combine targeted subsidies with student choice of institutions. Fees at higher education institutions must be combined with student loan and scholarship programs to ensure that all who wish to borrow for their education are able to do so and to guarantee necessary financial support to academically qualified poor students. When the University of the Philippines raised tuition fees in the late 1980s, for example, it also provided a special fund to support qualified students from low-income families.

Special Measures

Special measures are needed to increase the enrollments of girls, of the poor, of linguistic minorities, and of special populations. As poor parents do not always appreciate the value of educating their children, and many parents do not see the value of educating their daughters, investing in parents' education can be an important mechanism for increasing child schooling. Social marketing or awareness campaigns can help overcome lack of knowledge; examples are the community female education awareness program in Bangladesh (see box 8.1), the Pacto Pela Infancia in Brazil for disadvantaged children, and the program in Guatemala to promote daughters' education among fathers. Changes in the location, schedule, staffing, content, or direct costs of education can make schooling more relevant to social and material conditions (Colletta and Perkins 1995). Such measures include recruiting more women teachers and more teachers from the local community.

Girls

Parents in many countries would like their girls to be taught by women, and a shortage of female teachers can inhibit school attendance. In Kerala state, which has the highest female literacy and enrollment rates in India, more than 60 percent of teachers are women, compared with less than 20 percent in Bihar and Uttar Pradesh, the two states with the lowest enrollment rates for girls. Not having a school within easy reach of home also deters girls' enrollment because of parents' concerns about girls' safety. In Morocco the presence of a paved road increases by 40 percent the chance of a girl ever attending school and reduces the probability of her dropping out by 5 percent. Too often, girls do not go to school because of the lack of separate lavatories and common rooms. In some cultures girls' participation in school depends on whether single-sex schools are available.

The basic policy instrument for expanding girls' enrollments is to increase school places for them. This can be done by reserving places and by expanding enrollments. If there are too few places, those available often go to boys. In Malawi one-third of all secondary school places are reserved for girls, and a Bank-assisted project to build secondary schools resulted in higher female enrollments than expected. Tanzania and Zambia have similar policies. Bangladesh, Chad, India, Pakistan, Senegal, and Yemen have made special efforts to expand classrooms or build new schools for girls. In Bangladesh and India these improvements include women's colleges and polytechnics at the tertiary level, as well as at the primary and secondary levels. Evidence shows that in many cultures girls' enrollment and performance improve if they attend single-sex schools rather than coeducational schools (Lee and Lockheed 1990). Care should be taken, however, that there are no differences in curricula in such cases. Some projects in Bangladesh and Pakistan are also providing separate sanitary facilities and constructing boundary walls around girls' schools. Locating schools within easy access of children's homes can lessen parents' concerns about girls' personal safety and reduce the direct costs of transport and boarding. Morocco is providing small local schools for middle-level education.

Other ways to increase girls' enrollment are to provide female teachers and childcare centers and to adjust school hours to fit girls' schedules. Cross-country data suggest a strong positive correlation between the parity of enrollment for boys and girls and the proportion of female teachers (Psacharopoulos and Tzannatos 1992). Initiatives in World Bank projects to overcome the shortage of female teachers, especially in rural areas, include implementing a quota system to recruit more female teachers, removing age restrictions, recruiting and posting teachers locally, and building teacher-training institutions in rural areas. Experience from Bangladesh, Pakistan, and Nepal suggests that it is not hard to find good female teachers if required training is provided and teachers are posted near their homes. The combination of locally recruited and motivated women teachers and active in-service training and supervision can reduce the shortage of women teachers in rural areas. Ongoing Bank-financed projects in Bangladesh, China, India, Nepal, Pakistan, and Yemen are testing such strategies for increasing the proportion of female teachers.

Childcare centers at or near schools and flexible hours can free girls to attend school. Childcare provision relieves girls from sibling care during the day and, when accompanied by nutrition programs, can help improve the health and school readiness of younger siblings. In Colombia, where single mothers head one-fifth of the poorest households and where 44 percent of poor children between ages 7 and 11 do not attend school, the community day-care program has freed many girls and women to attend school or join the work force. Adjusting school hours so that girls can more easily combine schooling with chores has also worked well in many countries, particularly in Nepal (World Bank 1994b).

Special Populations

The principal policy instrument for reducing the high incidence of physical and learning impairments in developing countries is improvement of child nutrition and health. Special programs to improve the nutrition and health of schoolchildren can help increase access to and equity in schools. For example, school feeding programs can be designed to have a differential impact on the enrollment and participation of girls, as in Ghana. Other programs, such as the treatment of parasites and micronutrient fortification or supplementation—both of which are relatively inexpensive and easy to implement—can significantly improve the disadvantaged child's ability to take advantage of educational opportunities. Educating children with minor impairments does not usually require costly facilities or programs. In India, for example, an Integrated Education for the Disabled project led to the identification and education of more than 13,000 children with special educational needs at a unit cost comparable to that of regular education (World Bank 1994j). Disabilities affect about 140 million children, about 15 percent of whom could have their sight, movement, or hearing enhanced at a unit cost of $25-$40 (Mittler 1992). Unit costs for special education can be reduced by using community-based approaches, which also create better opportunities for children. Community-based rehabilitation programs exist in many countries, including India, Indonesia, Jamaica, Kenya, Malaysia, Nepal, the Philippines, and Zimbabwe. Costs can be shared with nongovernmental organizations, as in Indonesia, where the public education system provides 45 percent of the resources for special education and private voluntary agencies provide the other 55 percent (World Bank 1994j).

Language Diversity

In multilingual nations, reading comprehension is often greater for students taught in bilingual schools, who first learn to read in their native language and then transfer their reading skills to the second language. More than 40 percent of Guatemalans entering school do not know Spanish. In 1979 Guatemala established a national bilingual education program, with USAID and World Bank support, to improve the quality of education for the indigenous population. The national curriculum was adapted and translated into four Mayan languages for the preprimary level through grade 4. The program has led to an increase in student comprehension and has reduced student failure, repetition, and dropout rates compared with a control group of Mayan children being taught only in Spanish. Bilingual program students score higher in all subjects, including Spanish, and have a promotion rate 9 percent higher (World Bank

1994d). Bilingual education also has the support of the children's parents and so increases the demand for education (Richards and Richards 1990).

Effective schools in multilingual societies may be those that are permitted flexibility in language of instruction (Eisemon 1989; Eisemon, Ratzlaff, and Patel 1992). The implementation of language policies should not be prescribed by national authorities, at least at the primary level. There, the focus should be on language learning outcomes and perhaps on the establishment of general objectives for the use of the mother tongue and other languages at particular grade levels and for particular subjects. Implementation should be a local, preferably school-level, responsibility. Institutional autonomy makes local implementation easier, since local schools and communities know their own circumstances best.

Other Disadvantaged Groups

Special attention is also needed to ensure equity of access to other disadvantaged groups, such as nomads, those who live in geographically remote regions, street children, and refugees. Strategies must vary from country to country, and nonformal methods will often be more appropriate than formal schooling. Particularly troublesome is the growing number of refugee children in Africa; many of them have no government to take the responsibility for providing them with schooling.

CHAPTER NINE

Household Involvement

EDUCATIONAL institutions may be more accountable for their performance when households are more closely involved in the institutions that family members attend. Parents involved with a school are more likely to be satisfied and, even more important, to help make it more effective. Most households already contribute, directly or indirectly, to the costs of education, but they could participate in school management and oversight, along with their wider communities, and they could be given the possibility of choosing among schools.

School Governance

Around the world, parents and communities are becoming more involved in the governance of their children's schools, just as students are in their higher education institutions. Sri Lanka furnishes one example (box 9.1). The elected boards of trustees that manage schools in New Zealand are drawn from parents of children at the school. In Mauritius parent-teacher associations have been so successful that government funds are now being used to stimulate the partnership further. Many countries have found that communities which participate in school management are more willing to assist in the financing of schooling. Jamaica has set up a major program to stimulate this tendency; Bangladesh's

BOX 9.1   SCHOOL DEVELOPMENT BOARDS IN SRI LANKA

Legislation enacted in 1993 in Sri Lanka established school development boards (SDBs) with the purpose of promoting community participation in school management (Commonwealth Secretariat 1994). Each SDB consists of representatives from the school staff, parents, past students, and well-wishers and is chaired by the school principal. Acting through ten subcommittees, the SDB decides on and implements programs for the school's development. The ten subcommittees are:

■ Educational development (improvement of academic curricula and modes of teaching)

■ Co-curricular activities (promotion of extracurricular activities)

■ Moral development (promotion of cultural, religious, and moral activities)

■ Physical resources (infrastructure development)

■ Library and educational equipment (facilities improvement)

■ Schoolbooks, midday meals, and uniforms (deciding on school requirements)

■ Welfare and community relations (strengthening welfare activities)

■ Communications (interaction with media and the community)

■ Finance (utilization and disbursement of school funds)

■ Student personality development (development of the personality of the pupils and the school).

Social Mobilization Campaign, which involves the community in education, has been accompanied by a reactivation of school management committees throughout the country. El Salvador has started to involve communities in rural school management, with significant results in improved teacher attendance. Student achievement levels are comparable with those at traditional schools, even though the students tend to come from poor backgrounds.

Effective involvement in school governance does not come easily, however. New Zealand realized after it had embarked on its reform that intensive training was necessary for the newly elected parent trustees. Jamaica is training parents to help manage schools. Botswana found it very difficult to attract sufficiently qualified people to lower-secondary school boards of governors, especially in rural areas. Training can be effective both in literate communities, such as New Zealand, and in relatively illiterate ones, as in parts of Uganda. ActionAid in Uganda is providing community training in two districts for parent-teacher associations and school management committees.

School Choice

Several countries have a long tradition of parental choice. The Netherlands has had it throughout the whole twentieth century. In poor African countries such as Uganda there has always been complete freedom of choice for parents.

Increased experimentation with parental choice is another hallmark of recent educational reforms, particularly in Australia, Chile, England, the Netherlands, New Zealand, Sweden, and the United States. This trend reflects both a more market-oriented perspective on education, in which consumers (parents and students) choose among suppliers (schools and institutions), and the "choosiness" of a growing number of parents and students, who will no longer accept being assigned to a particular public school but want to make their own decisions (OECD 1994b). For choice to be an effective concept, the following factors are important.

■ The student must have within reach either more than one possible school or institution or multiple programs within a single institution.

■ The institutions should have some distinguishing characteristics.

■ Schools and institutions need to enjoy considerable autonomy in how they teach.

Diversity among institutions or programs can take the shape of differing emphases in the curriculum, styles of teaching, higher-level course offerings, and ownership (public or private). The existence of a variety of types of programs and institutions makes it possible for parents and students to exercise some choice, which in turn should give an incentive for providing quality education cost-effectively. This strategy is most relevant at the upper-secondary and higher levels of education, where choice among institutions can help to meet the growing unmet enrollment demand.

In higher education, for instance, choice among institutions of different types will typically imply the development of nonuniversity tertiary institutions and the encouragement of private and public institutions. Higher education institutions are much more varied in high-income countries than in low- and middle-income ones. Differentiation among developing countries is most extensive and effective in Asia. In East Asia, for example, the average annual growth of university enrollments between 1980 and 1988 was 6 percent, but for nonuniversity institutions it was 10 percent. The principal advantages of nonuniversity institutions are lower program costs (reflecting shorter courses), lower dropout rates, and lower per student annual costs. In Bulgaria average costs at universities are 15 percent more than at the higher institutes and 95 percent more than at the technical institutes. Nonuniversity institutions also offer training opportunities that respond flexibly to labor market demand rather than to supply-side factors. World Bank–assisted projects support the differentiation of higher education. In Tunisia, for instance, a project is helping to establish a network of two-year technology institutions.

Greater separation of teaching and research will promote differences among and reduce costs at public universities. Much scientific research requires expensive scientific equipment, and there are undoubted benefits from concentrating efforts at a few institutions. The prevailing assumption that every public university should conduct research therefore needs to be reexamined.

Effective choice also means having private as well as public schools available. Most countries permit private schools, but some, including Algeria, Latvia, Syria, and, until recently, Pakistan, do not. Other countries excessively regulate the establishment and operation of private schools and universities. In Nigeria, for instance, it takes well over a year to go through the cumbersome bureaucratic process for establishing a private school. The proprietor must meet many ostensibly reasonable requirements (for example, showing that the school will be nonprofit and that there are sufficient resources to operate it for a specified period, posting a bond, and so on), but the real purpose is to put difficulties in the way of establishing private schools.

The ideal is a positive regulatory framework. In higher education such structures—in place in Colombia, Kenya, and Romania, for example—provide an appropriate legal basis and accreditation system for both private and public universities. In some countries, such as Chile, students may enroll at the primary and secondary level in public or private institutions of the parents' choice; the state provides the funds.

Another factor in ensuring effective household decisionmaking is educational institutions' autonomy in how they teach. This freedom is related to the second factor, since autonomy permits different combinations of inputs that in turn produce institutions with distinct characteristics. Private schools are autonomous; public ones can be but often are not. Indeed, management differences at the school level are probably one reason why private secondary schools in a study of five developing countries appear to provide more learning for the same cost as public ones (table 9.1), even after controlling for the socioeconomic backgrounds of the students. Private schools per se are not necessarily more effective than public ones, however. In the Indian state of Tamil Nadu government-aided schools are more cost-effective in raising student achievement in mathematics and reading, but fully private unaided schools are less cost-effective than public schools. School management practices in government-aided schools—notably, instructional management by the principal, the quality of textbooks, training for teachers in how to use textbooks, and the availability of instructional materials—go far to explain their better perfor-

TABLE 9.1   RELATIVE AVERAGE COST AND EFFICIENCY OF PUBLIC AND PRIVATE SCHOOLS, EARLY 1980S

Country	Ratio of private cost to public cost	Ratio of relative effectiveness to cost	Ratio of relative cost to effectiveness
Colombia	0.69	1.64	0.61
Dominican Republic	0.65	2.02	0.50
Philippines	0.83	1.20	0.83
Tanzania	0.69	1.68	0.59
Thailand	0.39	6.74	0.17

Source: Lockheed and Jimenez 1994.

mance (Bashir 1994). School-level management, not private or public status, is what can affect outcomes and hence provide real choice to households.

Risks

Although there is a long tradition of school choice in many countries, little systematic research into its effects has been done to date. As yet, no evidence exists that the competition among schools and programs implicit in the concept of school choice improves or worsens school performance. However, "the dynamic of competing for pupils typically enhances some school characteristics associated with effectiveness, such as strong leadership and sense of mission" (OECD 1994b). This finding points in the direction of further cautious experimentation in focusing increased household involvement on school choice. (No such ambiguity exists with regard to increased involvement in school governance.)

Increased household involvement carries several risks. It can make carrying out systemwide education policies and enforcing broader national objectives more difficult. Social segregation can also increase if the education system becomes polarized between prestigious schools for the academically able children of educated parents and schools with less impressive credentials for the children of the poor and uneducated. Equity can be reduced if schools and institutions start accepting students on the basis of their ability to pay rather than on their academic entrance qualifications.

These risks can be mitigated relatively easily through policies for the provision of public funding and, as in the Netherlands, through limits on fees at schools that receive public funds. Public finance for public schools or to assist private schools can be restricted to schools that follow certain overall policies, such as adhering to a national curriculum and practicing nondiscriminatory enrollment policies, in addition to meeting basic health and safety requirements. Public finance for the education of children from poorer backgrounds can be provided at a higher unit level than for children from better-off socioeconomic groups, as is the practice in New Zealand, for instance. Public financing or provision of transport to school can be adjusted so that it is not difficult for a child to attend a school other than that nearest to the family home.

Another risk is that parents may not have enough information to make effective judgments about quality. Many studies show that parents' decisions about schools are not made principally on the basis of well-informed comparisons of educational quality (OECD 1994b). Although this risk can never be completely overcome, it can be mitigated through the provision of open and independent information about school quality. It is appropriate for the government to supply such information, since there is an information asymmetry between the education system and households: school administrators have access to performance and financial data that is unavailable to students and parents. The British government provides inspection reports and examination results in a form that is designed to be meaningful to parents. In the United States the Boston school system, having broken the link between place of residence and assignment of public school places, has set up information centers to assist parents in making decisions among public schools. Since school choice was introduced in Sweden, schools have prepared information on curricula and finances. Governments in low- and middle-income countries may not be able to emulate all these practices, but they could make available information from national examinations and from the national assessment systems that are increasingly being introduced. Kenya's Ministry of Education, for instance, publishes a table ranking the performance of secondary schools on national examinations.

CHAPTER TEN

Autonomous Institutions

Educational quality can increase when schools are able to use instructional inputs according to local school and community conditions and when they are accountable to parents and communities. Increased household involvement to increase accountability was discussed in chapter 9. If effective use is to be made of instructional inputs, institutions must be autonomous. Such a strategy is relevant in all contexts, even remote rural areas. Fully autonomous educational institutions have authority to allocate their resources (not necessarily to raise them), and they are able to create an educational environment adapted to local conditions inside and outside the school.

It is important to note that school autonomy is not the same as either local financing or administrative decentralization, although the three are often confused. Local financing of education means that resources are raised locally, which can create problems of equity among richer and poorer localities. Decentralization is simply assignment of responsibility for education to an institution or level of government other than the central government. Institutional autonomy can be encouraged by both administrative and financial means.

Administrative Measures

To obtain the necessary flexibility, school managements (principals and governing bodies) must have authority to allocate resources. This includes the authority to deploy personnel and to determine such things as the timing of the school day, the duration of the school year, and the language of instruction, to fit local conditions. Such authority will increase the efficiency of learning. Teachers must have authority to determine classroom practices—within limits set by a broad national curriculum, encouraged by examinations, and monitored and supported by standards, learning assessments, and school inspectors. Finally, school staff must be accountable to the local community.

So long as schools are solely accountable to central bureaucracies, they will be organized in a management structure that limits school autonomy (Hannaway 1991). This framework reduces incentives to respond to parental and community concerns about school performance and costs, and it curbs schools' capacity to respond because clearances must be sought before schools can proceed with changes in their operations. This is true for countries at all income levels. However, schools in low- and middle-income countries are much less autonomous than those in high-income countries (tables 10.1 and 10.2). Relatively fewer decisions are made by principals and teachers, and too often, decisions are made without appropriate input from local authorities (Lockheed, Verspoor, and others 1991; OECD 1993).

Local financing and decentralization can contribute to autonomy and accountability, but this does not happen automatically, as recent experience in Nicaragua, India, Chile and Russia demonstrates. As part of decentralization, the Nicaraguan Ministry of Education transfers funds to municipalities, which then hire, fire, and pay teachers. The potential benefit of this move has been nullified, however, by a law that stipulates a national teacher pay scale and by the insufficiency of the funds transferred from the ministry. Neither schools nor municipalities gain autonomy through such an arrangement. They do gain autonomy under a more promising reform: Nicaragua is transferring public secondary schools to private associations. To date, 20 of the country's 350 secondary schools have been transferred.

Amendments to the Indian constitution in 1992 shifted authority, including responsibility for education, to locally elected bodies (revived Panchayati Raj institutions) at the village, intermediate, and district levels within states. In response, teachers in Andhra Pradesh state successfully petitioned to become state employees, to limit the authority that the panchayats will be able to exercise over them.

After local financing was introduced, public spending on education declined 17 percent a year in Chile in 1985–90 and 9 percent a year in Mexico in 1982–90 (Prawda 1993). Local financing is also lowering spending in Russia as the federal government transfers responsibility downward.

As these examples show, it is critical to the improvement of learning that resources not be reduced when local management and financing of schools are increased. Measures are needed to ensure that adequate resources are available to each school if local financing is adopted. The purpose of increasing school

TABLE 10.1   LOCUS OF DECISIONMAKING AUTHORITY IN PRIMARY EDUCATION SYSTEMS IN SELECTED DEVELOPING COUNTRIES

(percent)

Type of decision and deciding body	Rep. of Korea	Philippines	Nigeria
Authorizing major expenditures			
Central or regional body	9	66	42
School board	78	7	33
School principal	11	5	1
Teachers	0	0	0
Selecting principals			
Central or regional body	40	83	38
School board	39	3	45
School principal	0	0	0
Teachers	0	0	1
Selecting teachers			
Central or regional body	6	63	37
School board	71	7	49
School principal	3	14	1
Teachers	0	1	0
Determining the range or type of science courses			
Central or regional body	61	82	82
School board	3	0	5
School principal	5	5	5
Teachers	28	5	5
Choosing science texts			
Central or regional body	89	76	59
School board	5	1	12
School principal	1	2	9
Teachers	1	0	6

Note: Percentages are based on the responses of teachers and school administrators to questions about decisionmaking authority. The four categories of decisionmaker do not include all the options, so percentages may not total 100.
Source: Lockheed, Verspoor, and others 1991, table 5-1.

autonomy is to permit flexibility in the combination of inputs and hence improve quality—not to save resources. For this reason, institutional autonomy need not involve local generation of resources but only local control over their allocation.

TABLE 10.2   DECISIONS MADE AT THE SCHOOL LEVEL AS A SHARE OF ALL DECISIONS BY PUBLIC SCHOOLS IN OECD COUNTRIES, BY LEVEL OF EDUCATION, 1991

(percent)

Level of education	Primary	Lower secondary	Upper secondary
Austria	44	44	47
Belgium	29	26	26
Denmark	39	39	42
Finland	41	38	59
France	17	35	35
Germany	32	32	32
Ireland	50	74	74
New Zealand	73	72	79
Norway	31	31	26
Portugal	33	42	42
Spain	28	28	28
Sweden	47	47	47
Switzerland[a]	9	9	23
United States	26	26	26

a. Almost all education decisions in Switzerland are made at the lowest level of government, the canton.
Source: OECD 1993.

Autonomy and accountability leading to flexibility also require that schools be allowed to manage themselves in ways that create conditions conducive to learning. For example, flexible use of multigrade teaching, at the option of the individual school, has been largely responsible for the success of the Escuelas Nuevas in Colombia, in which flexible techniques are applied to the formal education system. Similarly, with the program of the Bangladesh Rural Advancement Committee (box 10.1), flexibility has been effective on a large scale outside the formal system.

There is an important place for increased teacher involvement in decisionmaking in schools. Teacher participation will improve learning quality, but only as long as it is explicitly focused on instruction (Smylie 1994). Such a focus requires some outside influence and direction (David and Peterson 1984; Shavelson 1981). Without such direction, teachers' energies are likely to be diverted to areas at best only tangentially related to instruction (Hannaway 1993). The best external direction for focusing teachers on instruction is a national or regional curriculum.

Clusters of schools, sometimes called nucleos or school learning cells, facilitate professional interaction among teachers and decisionmaking about instruction. Indeed, professional interaction may be more important than

BOX 10.1   INVOLVEMENT OF NGOS
IN EDUCATION: THE BRAC STORY

In diversifying the supply of education in Bangladesh, the government has recognized the contribution nongovernmental organizations (NGOs) can make to efforts to expand access and improve the quality of education for the country's children. NGOs already play a national role in Bangladesh's health and population programs.

The Bangladesh Rural Advancement Committee (BRAC), the largest NGO in Bangladesh, is well known for its rural development, credit, and health programs. In 1985, in response to requests from participants in its rural development programs, BRAC started the nonformal primary education (NFPE) program for 8-to-10-year-olds in twenty-two villages. Girls were given special emphasis. By late 1991, 6,003 schools, serving 11-to-16-year-olds as well as the NFPE age group, had been established. The program is free to students, except for community contributions for school construction.

In 1992 more than 8,000 schools were operating, and plans are being implemented to expand the NFPE program to 50,000 schools nationwide by 1995. Throughout, BRAC has been able to balance its expansion program with its quality goals.

Internationally, BRAC is a model for the potential of the nongovernmental sector in educational expansion. It also illustrates how a combination of targeting, school design, flexibility, and follow-through can dramatically increase girls' primary-school participation rates. While national education systems everywhere have the formal mandate to provide quality education to their populaces, such NGOs as BRAC, which have greater flexibility than government bureaucracies, may sometimes be able to reach target groups more effectively. Furthermore, BRAC's expansion program illustrates that NGOs need not necessarily be limited to small pilot projects but can also carry out larger-scale delivery programs (Ahmed and others 1993).

---

decisionmaking authority for the motivation, learning, and social control of teachers' work (Hannaway 1993). Periodic conferences or workshops can provide opportunities for teachers representing different clusters to share what they are doing with their colleagues. School clusters have been used successfully in Costa Rica to develop new curricular materials in local languages and in India and Sri Lanka to share demonstration lessons among teachers (Bray 1987).

Financial Measures

Public finance can be used to encourage autonomy and accountability. The standard pattern of public education financing is to raise revenues through general taxes and to allocate expenditure centrally, through direct payments for inputs such as teachers' salaries and textbooks. The more that schools themselves can control the allocation of resources, however, the greater the possibilities of effective schooling. And the more that households are involved, the greater will be the incentives for the schools to improve quality.

Public finance mechanisms for achieving these purposes include the use of local rather than central government taxation; cost-sharing with local communities; the use of block grants; the charging of fees at higher levels of education; the encouragement of revenue diversification; the use of "portable" capitation grants, vouchers, and student loans; and funding based on output and quality. A variety of mechanisms are available for specific circumstances and levels of education.

Local Taxation

Funding of education through local taxes can increase the accountability of schools and institutions to parents and students. Local taxes are often used to fund school systems; in the United States, for instance, local property taxes are usually the principal source of revenues for school districts. There are two principal drawbacks to the use of local revenues for education. First, local governments may have less capacity than national ones to administer tax systems. Second, localities vary in their resource mobilization capacities, and this can lead to different per student funding levels and to inequalities in access, quality, retention, and learning outcomes.

The advantages of cost-sharing with local communities have already been discussed. This subject is particularly relevant at present in Eastern Europe, where responsibility for education at the primary and secondary levels is being transferred from central to state and local governments at the same time as fiscal federalism is being introduced. Revenue-sharing formulas could be adopted, as in Australia, to offset differences in state governments' fiscal capacities. Local funding is not essential to increased accountability, however; local control of centrally financed expenditure can have the same effect.

Block Grants

In Australia primary education is principally a state responsibility, but central government funds are allocated redistributively to states and districts on a per student basis in direct relation to the relative poverty of the district. In New Zealand the central government provides grants for operating costs directly to the school; the funds are administered by a locally elected board of trustees. Such mechanisms permit local control of resources for education without placing all the burden of resource mobilization on the local community or government. They can also offset differences in the socioeconomic status of students. In New Zealand, for instance, 80 percent of school funding is related to the number of students and 20 percent to the students' socioeconomic status. Poorer students thus attend schools that receive more funding per student.

Fees

Charging fees can create accountability between parents and students and school managements at the higher levels of education. Scholarships can be used to encourage enrollment of students from low-income families. Even at the primary level, the charging of fees need not be incompatible with the principle of free primary education, so long as those fees are regulated and are met by parents out of vouchers financed by the state, as is now done in Chile.

Revenue Diversification

Encouraging public educational institutions to diversify their sources of revenue and allowing them to keep such revenues can encourage autonomy. The scope for this is greatest in higher education. The practice of attracting resources from alumni and private industry is standard among private schools and universities and is beginning to spread to public ones. The University of the West Indies, for instance, has in recent years obtained alumni funding to establish a scholarship fund. In Chile, Indonesia, Thailand, and Venezuela private industry provides scholarships or subsidized loans for talented university students. Tax regimes can encourage such donations. In India 100 percent of individual and corporate contributions to universities are tax-deductible; in Chile, 50 percent.

Public schools and universities can also use their facilities to provide income. Universities in Uganda and Senegal generate 4 to 5 percent of annual expenditure by renting out facilities (Ziderman and Albrecht 1995). China, Mongolia, and Viet Nam encourage schools to rent out premises, run short courses, and provide services to industry. Such income amounts to 5 percent of the Mongolian education budget, 12 percent of the Chinese higher education budget and 14 percent of the Vietnamese budget (Wu 1993; Tsang 1993; Ziderman and Albrecht 1995).

"Portable" Student Funding

Capitation grants, vouchers, and loans have the potential to encourage autonomy and competition, but experience with these mechanisms is limited. All operate under the same principle: the state makes available to the student a voucher or loan, which the student may then use to pay for his or her education at any institution, public or private. These mechanisms thus finance the demand side of education, encouraging a marketplace in which suppliers must meet the demand. They establish a situation in which public subsidies increase the educational purchasing power of poor students and put them in the same situation relative to the providers of education as those who pay for their higher education from their own or family funds.

Primary and secondary education in Chile is now financed publicly through the use of capitation grants; parents may enroll their children at any private or public school, and the school then receives funding from the government according to the number who enroll. Since the system was introduced in the early 1980s, it has led to a major increase in the number of private schools and to increased private school enrollment. In the Netherlands parents have the right to a free primary and secondary education for their children at any public or religious private school of their choosing, and the schools are funded by capitation grants on the basis of enrollments. Preschool education in New Zealand is funded by the state on the basis of a fixed sum per student, which can be received by any accredited institution or person. In the United States, Minnesota allows public high school students in their final year to enroll in postsecondary institutions (with tax funds being paid to the institutions) and permits enrollments outside the school district in which the student lives. A few experiments with voucher schemes have been tried in World Bank–financed projects, as in Colombia and Pakistan (for girls), but evaluation is still at an early stage.

In Hungary, Indonesia, Mongolia, Nigeria, and Viet Nam public higher education institutions are funded on the basis of enrollment figures, with allowances for different unit costs for different courses. Unless accompanied by limitations on admissions or on the number of students who can receive such funding, these schemes can, in theory, lead to open-ended budgetary commitments. They also fail to provide sufficient incentives for efficiency. While relatively small in that it covers only 6 percent of the student body, the Colombian student loan scheme is available to low-income students, and the loans are portable; they may be used to finance education at public and private institutions, not just in Colombia but also abroad.

Output-Based and Quality-Based Funding

Output-based schemes fund institutions by the number of graduates they produce, rather than the number of students they enroll. This reduces wastage and improves overall efficiency. Such schemes are relatively rare and are limited to higher education in Australia, Denmark, Finland, Israel, and the Netherlands. No developing country yet uses such a plan, although Brazil is moving in this direction. In the Netherlands universities receive 4.5 years of annual unit cost funding per graduate, regardless of how long it takes students to complete their studies. After the scheme was introduced, the graduation rate improved from 48 percent in 1980 to 80 percent in 1987.

Quality-based funding has been tried in only one country, Chile. Higher education institutions receive a financial award from the government for each entering student who scored among the top 27,500 in the university aptitude test. The objective of this scheme is to stimulate competition among institutions to improve their quality and thus to attract the best students, although it runs the risk of favoring those institutions that attract students from the highest socio-economic groups. In Hungary the World Bank is supporting reform of higher education through a "fund for new initiatives," access to which is competitive on the basis of institutions' proposals to strengthen the quality, efficiency, and relevance of their programs. Research has been funded in this way in World Bank–assisted projects in Brazil, China, Egypt, and Korea.

Risks

In higher education the benefits of autonomy are clear. At the school level, some caution is needed. Among the countries that have experimented most with increasing school autonomy in recent years are Chile, New Zealand, and the United Kingdom. In all three, there is still little evidence available on how the increased school-level flexibility that has resulted from autonomy has affected overall quality.

The risks of school-level autonomy arise particularly with regard to inequalities in educational opportunities and adherence to national standards and the curriculum. They can be largely mitigated by clearly separating school-level management and control over resource allocation from exclusive reliance on local financing and by ensuring that some functions are maintained external to the school, at the national or regional level. Among the particularly important tasks in this category are standard setting; development of curricula and performance assessment mechanisms, such as public examinations and learning assessments; and use of national mechanisms to offset regional inequalities in resources if schools are funded locally. The curriculum and the financing of education have not been left to the school or even to the local level in any of these three pioneering countries.

PART III

Implementing Change

IN MOST COUNTRIES vested interests are roadblocks to financial and managerial change in education. For both governments and the World Bank, a sectoral approach, rooted in country circumstances, is essential. For countries, a sectoral approach implies working for maximum efficiency in the allocation and use of resources so as to improve the quality and increase the quantity of education. For the World Bank, a sectoral approach implies, in addition to those improvements in quality and quantity that Bank lending supports directly, attention to the policy environment and to institution building so that Bank financing and assistance help develop the sector as a whole.

In all countries Bank lending will be concerned with the policy environment and with the creation and strengthening of institutions. The subsectoral allocation of lending will usually follow countries' own resource allocation priorities. Primary and lower-secondary education will therefore continue to receive the highest priority in the Bank's education lending to countries that have not yet achieved universal literacy and adequate access, equity, and quality at these levels. In some cases it may be necessary to adjust the rate of increase of enrollments in order to ensure that the quality of schooling keeps pace with them. In the countries that have yet to achieve universal literacy, the Bank's involvement in higher education will continue to be confined mainly to making the financing of higher education more equitable and cost-effective so that primary and secondary education can receive increased resources.

As the basic education system develops in coverage and effectiveness, more attention can be devoted to the upper-secondary and higher levels. Bank lending for higher education will support countries' efforts to adopt policy reforms that will allow the subsector to operate more efficiently and at lower public cost. Countries prepared to adopt a higher education policy framework that stresses a differentiated institutional structure and a diversified resource base, with greater emphasis on private providers and private funding, will continue to receive priority.

The transition economies of Eastern and Central Europe form a special category. Their primary and secondary enrollment ratios are high, but they need to adjust the entire education system toward the needs of a market economy. Particularly important are efforts to maintain funding levels for compulsory (primary and secondary) education; to shift away from overspecialization in vocational, technical, and higher education institutions; and to reform the governance and financing of higher education. In many ways, reform of higher education is the key starting point for much of the broader sectoral reform that is involved for these economies.

CHAPTER ELEVEN

The Political and Social Context of Change

REFORMS of education, whatever their technical merit, will not take hold unless they are politically and socially acceptable and unless the pace of reform is appropriate. Education is intensely political because it affects the majority of citizens, involves all levels of government, is almost always the single largest component of public spending, and carries public subsidies that are biased in favor of the elite. Prevailing systems of education expenditure and management often protect the interests of teachers' unions, university students, the elite, and the central government at the expense of parents, communities, and the poor. The pace of reform must therefore take account of those vested interests and also of the need for adequate resources to sustain the reform. (The appendix to this chapter discusses reform priorities in the special case of the transition economies.)

Teachers are usually the single largest group of civilian public employees in developing countries. Because educational finance and management are typically the responsibility of central government, teachers' unions are important actors on the national political stage. In Latin America, Eastern Europe, and some Asian countries, for instance, they have established their own political parties or have formed alliances with parties representing trade union movements. When governments fail to reach agreement with strong central unions over conditions of employment for teachers, collective action can disrupt education and sometimes lead to political paralysis, as has happened in Bolivia, Peru, and other countries in recent years.

The relationship between higher education students and the government can be oppositional, as well. The conflict arises because of the centralized nature of university financing and governance and because higher education students, who come disproportionately from upper socioeconomic households, are a vocal and articulate political constituency. When students have grievances, usually only national governments can address them. In Romania in 1993, for instance, university students besieged the national Ministry of Education and the parliament to protest overcrowding in student hostels. In Africa heads of state are usually university chancellors, institutionalizing the potential for political opposition when students have grievances. In Kenya and Uganda students have several times brought before ministers and the head of state complaints about the food served in cafeterias and the introduction of tuition charges. Such action has often precipitated political crisis and university closures. Changing the centralized pattern of university finance and administration can ease the oppositional relationship between students and the government.

Whereas teachers and higher education students are politically influential as a result of centralized patterns of education finance and management, parents and communities are relatively weak. In most developing countries since the end of the colonial period, national governments have assumed responsibility for education systems, at least at the primary level. They have taken up this role with the best of intentions: to overcome the inequities that characterized the preindependence pattern of private, voluntary, and local education; to widen social access to education; and to build "nationalism" through a single government-controlled curriculum. Emphasis on these goals has come at the cost of shifting responsibility away from communities and parents. Where there is a tradition of local responsibility, the education system can be very responsive to parents and communities. In the Indian state of Kerala, for instance, almost all schools have active parent-teacher associations that involve parents in school management, noon feeding programs, fund raising, and facilities development.

The proelite bias of public spending on education, particularly tertiary education, makes reform difficult. The relatively affluent are naturally loath to give up their privileges, as has been shown in many countries when governments have introduced or increased fees at public universities and other higher education institutions.

Successful reform of education finance and management requires a significant expansion of educational opportunities, extensive consultation with current and potential stakeholders, mechanisms to increase the say of parents and communities in the system, and thorough design of the reforms that includes public finance. Education financing and management changes are best introduced as educational opportunities are expanded (box 11.1). Sometimes the change itself does this, as when prohibitions on the private sector are lifted. The expansion of cost-sharing in public higher education, for instance, is politically

BOX 11.1   TRADEOFFS BETWEEN ACCESS
AND QUALITY: LESSONS FROM KENYA
AND THAILAND

Have expanding enrollments caused the quality of schooling to suffer? The evidence cited to support that assertion includes the poor academic performance of low- and middle-income country students, the high incidence of wastage and repetition, increasing reliance on untrained teachers, use of double shifts, and lower investments in critical learning inputs such as textbooks. In many countries, enrollments have expanded more rapidly than the financial and other resources that are needed to support greater school coverage while maintaining school quality.

This is particularly so in Sub-Saharan African countries, which traditionally had low gross enrollment ratios and which, since becoming independent, have given high priority to increasing access to schooling. In some of these countries primary-level enrollments have grown by 5 to 10 percent a year; in Kenya, for instance, primary school enrollments increased dramatically after tuition and other fees were gradually abolished beginning in 1974. In 1984–85 the duration of primary schooling was lengthened, and enrollment expanded by about 583,000 in one year.

Each such measure to increase participation and raise educational attainment has had deleterious implications for school financing and instruction. Ministerial task forces established to study the implications of the new eight-year primary cycle urged caution and gradualism, citing inadequate finance,

lack of trained teachers and facilities, and the need to prepare new curricula and textbooks. Nevertheless, the government hastily implemented the reform, although few schools outside Kenya's principal cities and towns could marshal the teaching and other instructional resources necessary for the new program of studies when it was introduced. More than 18,000 untrained teachers were eventually employed to enable schools to extend instruction by an additional year, setting back the significant progress that had been made since 1963 in providing primary schools with trained teachers (Eisemon 1988).

Educational access and attainment can be increased, with attention to school quality, when plans for expansion take account of implementation issues. In Thailand a similar reform, announced in 1988, would have lengthened compulsory schooling to nine years and integrated lower-secondary and primary schooling. After more careful consideration of what was required to successfully implement such a reform, the government decided to introduce the nine-year schools gradually. In the pilot phase 718 of these schools were established in 38 economically disadvantaged provinces. In 1990 the experiment was extended to 122 schools in 73 provinces, and it is expected that by 1996 the number of schools will have increased to 4,187, with an enrollment of 750,000. The schools are experimenting with the new curricula and textbooks and with new models of school management, including community involvement in designing the school program (Holsinger 1994).

most feasible when it is explicitly linked to the expansion of opportunities for higher education. In Chile and Hungary the reform of higher education was successful because overall enrollments increased. In Chile fees were introduced, and enrollments were increased through an expansion and differentiation of the higher education system and the introduction of student choice. A World Bank loan to Hungary is supporting a sweeping reform of the higher education system in which public institutions will start to raise fees and opportunities will expand. The reform involves the encouragement of private institutions and the direct funding of students at private and public institutions through a state student-grant fund and through loans.

In countries as diverse as Bolivia, the Dominican Republic, Ghana, Guinea, India, Jordan, Mauritius, Mozambique, Romania, and Thailand, education reform has made a good start because stakeholders have been involved in developing and implementing the reforms. In Bolivia and the Dominican Republic the UNDP has financed consultation mechanisms to encourage the development of national consensus around education reform. In both cases a reform policy document and an accompanying public investment program were endorsed by the teachers' union, parents' representatives, and the major political parties and were successfully presented at meetings of donors, including the World Bank. In Bolivia the reform program prepared by the previous government has remained intact since the opposition came to power in the 1993 election. In Ghana a process of national consultation extended from the head of state down to every community through a series of "town meetings." In Mauritius a far-reaching education master plan is being implemented, following an extensive process of public consultation (box 11.2). Less extensive processes have also proved useful in Jordan and Thailand, where reform committees included representatives of teachers' unions, education ministries, and school and university administrators, although parent and student involvement was more limited (Haddad 1994). Effective collaboration between government and teachers' unions to achieve reform has been demonstrated in several countries, including Ghana, Korea, Singapore, and Zimbabwe.

Reform is also successful when involvement by communities, parents, and students is increased. Community and parent control, when accompanied by measures to ensure equity in the provision of resources, can offset much of the power of vested interests, such as teachers' unions and the elite. Parent and community involvement can be increased by decentralization, school level autonomy, and accountability of the school to local people. At least in urban areas, it can be enhanced by the use of market mechanisms that increase accountability and choice. In both urban and rural areas it can also be enhanced by the use of participatory methods in designing and implementing reforms (Colleta and Perkins 1995).

BOX 11.2   STAKEHOLDER PARTNERSHIP
IN MAURITIUS

Mauritius is a multiracial, multilingual society whose education system had not changed significantly since the colonial period. In 1990 its minister of education began consultations on reform of the system. A steering committee, a working group, and sectoral subcommittees were created to collect opinions on the subject and hold public hearings to study options. Technical studies were commissioned, and a strategy paper was circulated for public debate. Special efforts were made to solicit the views of teachers on particularly contentious issues, such as their role in curriculum development and continuous assessment, in-service training, and performance evaluation. A televised national seminar was held on the reform plans to ensure countrywide participation and consultation.

The reform plan that emerged was adopted by the government with support from the World Bank and other donors. The plan will increase attain-ment, reduce wastage, and reduce variations in quality by lengthening the cycle of compulsory education to nine years, revising curricula and assessment practices, and strengthening school-level management. It will affect the powers and responsibilities of teachers and private schools, as well as many interests within the education bureaucracy, including the examinations syndicate, teacher training institutions, and various technical departments of the Ministry of Education.

"The intense internal struggle and strong opposition from some groups has not been reconciled," a recent evaluation of the reform process acknowledges. "The important shift introduced by this reform process, however, was to move educational policy-making from the close province of the professional educators (and government) to a more open forum involving parents, vested interests, lobbyists, unions, and the community at large." It is still too early to assess the impact of the reform itself, now being put into effect (Bhowon and Chinapah 1993).

It is important that reform efforts clearly define the new roles and responsibilities of the actors in the education system. Critically important here is the complementarity of policy reform and public finance. Half measures—too rapid policy reforms without financial mechanisms—do not work, as illustrated by decentralization in Ghana and the regulation of private institutions in Korea. In the colonial period Ghana had strong local governments with independent tax bases that provided high-quality primary education. Following years of centralized control after independence, recent reforms have returned the responsibility for financing basic education to local governments but without giving them the authority to raise revenue (Associates in Rural Development 1993). In Korea during the 1970s the government tried to influence the level and distribution of enrollments in private educational institutions through the accreditation process. It attempted to limit total private enrollments and to shift their balance toward science and engineering. Since public finance was not available to the private institutions, the government had no effective instrument for enforcing its policy, and the regulations were ultimately abandoned.

Appendix. Priorities for Educational Reform in Eastern and Central Europe

In Eastern and Central Europe, strategies for educational reform must anticipate the establishment of competitive market economies and pluralistic, legitimate, and stable political systems. These conditions hardly exist in many countries in the region. Large state-owned enterprises, for example, continue to provide most employment, and frequent changes in governments have inhibited economic and educational reform.

Radical reforms—including new curricula and innovative methods of instruction—are required in the management, financing, and structure of education to restore these countries to political and economic health. Comprehensive educational reforms will accelerate recovery, provide a long-term foundation for growth, and support development of democratic political and social institutions. The benefits of an open economy and a participatory political system cannot be captured by individuals without market and citizenship skills. National income would be very much higher if education were restructured now, without delay.

High priority should be placed on reform of compulsory education. The challenge is enormous. Real per pupil expenditures on compulsory schooling have been declining precipitously in most countries in the region, while enrollment has been stable or increasing. For example, in Russia per student expenditures on compulsory schooling decreased 29 percent between 1991 and 1992, although enrollment slightly increased. Investment in physical facilities dropped by 23 percent during this period and supplies of textbooks by 16 percent. Teacher salaries fell to about two-thirds of average industrial wages, prompting widespread teacher strikes that in 1992 accounted for the majority of all days lost to strikes.

In Russia and many other countries in the region, reforms are needed to protect compulsory education from fiscal instability and ensure equity at least in nonsalary expenditures as more responsibility for financing is devolved onto local government authorities. To promote democratization, local authorities and schools should have greater control of their budgets—for establishing teacher salaries and conditions of employment, for allocating expenditure be-

tween capital and recurrent costs, and for obtaining textbooks and other learning resources.

To accomplish this, the functions of national and local educational authorities will need to be re-examined. At the national level, transfer payment schemes
will have to be designed to take into account the different resource-generating
capacities of local governments and to promote fiscal effort and local initiative.
Mechanisms need to be developed at the national level to manage compulsory
education effectively, allowing variation in implementation at the local level.
The critical functions of national governments include setting curricular objectives for core subjects, formulating minimal standards for instructional facilities and the distribution of texts and learning resources, elaborating a regulatory
framework to facilitate the development of private education, monitoring student performance, and protecting the rights of linguistic and ethnic minorities.

Reforming the overspecialized programs of vocational, technical, and higher
education institutions will require even bolder initiatives. At the beginning of
the transition, a very high proportion of students in secondary and higher
education was enrolled in programs designed to supply to state-owned enterprises and public services graduates with specialized skills that the nascent
labor market cannot absorb. In Poland in 1990–91, 76 percent of secondary
school students were enrolled in vocational and technical programs. In Romania in 1989–90, about two-thirds of all higher education students were enrolled
in narrowly defined engineering programs. Vocational and technical schools,
which accounted for more than 80 percent of upper secondary enrollment,
offered 354 curricular specializations. In 1991, 50 percent of students enrolled
in secondary technical schools and 25 percent of those in vocational programs
were training in machine trades and metal work, although job vacancies in
these specialties represented only 5 percent of vacancy listings.

The number of students in specialized engineering, vocational, and technical programs has dropped sharply during the transition, and the distribution of
enrollment has shifted in response to student demand. For example, the proportion of students in engineering in Romanian universities declined from 65 to 38
percent between 1989–90 and 1992–93. Romania's higher education system
has experienced rapid growth in recent years. The majority of students are now
enrolled in foreign language programs, law, economics, management, and other
social sciences. But where little progress has been made in reforming the structure of secondary and higher education programs, total enrollments have usually declined, as has happened in Russia.

Governments in Eastern and Central Europe should give priority to expanding enrollment in general secondary education; to increasing the amount of
academic instruction students receive, especially in foreign languages; and to

introducing new subjects such as computer training that a competitive market economy requires. Above all, reforms should increase student choice, through promoting curricular flexibility in general programs and in vocational and technical programs, so that the system will react more rapidly to changes in employment opportunities.

At the higher level, government policies should encourage private provision and increased private financing of public higher education to stimulate competition, innovation, and responsiveness to the labor market. The political freedoms public universities obtained after the collapse of socialism should be accompanied by more autonomy in using public funds and in mobilizing additional resources. At the same time, governments should establish open, transparent mechanisms for allocating public funding, with incentives for improving efficiency and restructuring academic programs. New policy structures will also have to be created to ensure quality control of both public and private institutions and to guide the development of the higher education system as a whole (Eisemon and others 1995; Heyneman 1994; Laporte and Schweitzer 1994; Sadlak 1993; Spagat 1994; World Bank 1992, 1994k, 1994l).

CHAPTER TWELVE

The World Bank and Education

THE WORLD BANK is today the largest single source of external finance for education in developing countries, accounting for about a quarter of all external support (table 12.1). Since its first education project in 1963, the Bank has continuously expanded its financing of education projects, in both absolute and relative terms, as part of its mission to reduce poverty. Total lending for education over the past thirty years through fiscal 1994 amounts to $19.2 billion, through more than 500 projects in more than 100 countries. Lending commitments are currently around $2 billion each year.

Developments since 1980

Six major shifts characterize the decade and a half since the last World Bank education sector policy paper was issued, in 1980. The total volume of education lending has tripled, and its share in overall Bank lending has doubled. Primary and secondary education are increasingly important and in fiscal 1993 and 1994 represented half of all education lending. Lending, once concentrated in Africa, East Asia, and the Middle East, is now significant in all regions. Girls' education is receiving explicit emphasis. Bank funds are today used less for buildings and more for other educational inputs. A narrow project approach is increasingly giving way to a broad sectoral one.

TABLE 12.1   EXTERNAL SUPPORT FOR EDUCATION, 1975–90

Item	1975	1980	1985	1986	1987	1988	1989	1990
Amount (millions of dollars)								
Total	2,018	4,496	4,255	4,644	4,584	5,528	5,838	6,035
Bilateral	1,490	3,595	2,679	3,169	3,512	3,950	3,790	3,640
Multilateral	528	901	1,576	1,475	1,072	1,578	2,048	2,395
World Bank	224	440	928	829	440	864	964	1,487
World Bank share (percent)								
Of total support	11	10	22	18	10	16	17	25
Of multilateral support	42	49	59	56	41	55	47	62

Source: UNESCO 1993b.

Lending Volume

Lending for education has increased significantly since 1980, both in absolute terms and as a share of total World Bank lending (figure 12.1). In the early 1980s lending commitments for education averaged about $0.6 billion a year and represented 4 percent of total Bank lending. They have now tripled in volume, to about $2.0 billion a year, with annual fluctuations, and the share has doubled to more than 8 percent. These figures exclude project-related training included in Bank projects in other sectors. The Bank is strongly committed to continued support for education. A particularly interesting development in fiscal 1994 was the first education loan by the International Finance Corporation (IFC), to the private Rainbow Academy secondary school in Uganda.

Priorities within the Education Sector

Lending for primary education has grown rapidly since 1980, and particularly since the late 1980s (figure 12.2), reflecting the growing realization of the importance of this level of education for economic growth and the reduction of poverty, the influence of the 1990 policy paper on primary education, and the Bank's commitment to the objectives of the 1990 Education for All Conference. The Bank was one of the sponsors of the conference and continues to participate in Education for All follow-up activities. During fiscal 1990–94 a third of all Bank lending for education was for primary education, more than double the share a decade before, with an emphasis on both access and quality. Future lending plans indicate a likely continuation of this trend and an increase

FIGURE 12.1   WORLD BANK EDUCATION LENDING, FISCAL 1980–94

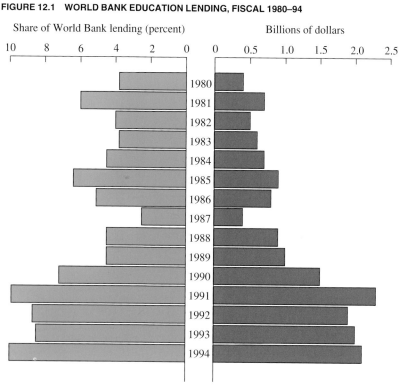

Source: World Bank Annual Report, various years.

in the share of secondary education. The emphasis on primary and secondary education has led to a slightly reduced share for higher education in overall lending. In addition, the Bank has in the 1990s started to lend for early child-hood development, including early childhood education, although these projects are still too new to be evaluated. Despite the major shifts in subsectoral empha-sis, the overall increase in lending volume has led to an absolute increase in lending for all subsectors, except vocational education, which has declined in both relative and absolute terms.

Primary education projects have focused on access, equity, internal effi-ciency, and quality. Access is being improved through projects that target poor regions, as in China and Mexico (box 12.1), and girls and minority groups, as in

FIGURE 12.2   WORLD BANK EDUCATION LENDING BY SUBSECTOR, FISCAL 1964–94

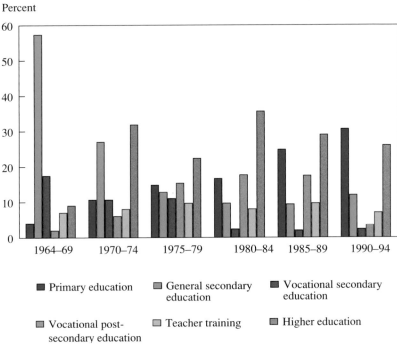

Percent

Source: World Bank data.

Bangladesh, India, Mexico, and Pakistan. Internal efficiency gains are the objective of projects that support increased student-teacher ratios (Barbados), multigrade schools (Colombia), double-shift teaching (Trinidad and Tobago), decentralization (Brazil), and community participation (Ghana). Quality improvements are supported by the development of national learning assessment systems, which are now included in 27 percent of primary school projects, compared with only 3 percent twenty years ago, and by an increased emphasis on important inputs other than school buildings, such as textbooks, laboratory equipment, and teacher training.

Lending for secondary education declined between 1980 and 1990, when it represented 10 percent of education lending. Since 1990, however, it has increased modestly, to 12 percent of all education lending, with 30 percent of education projects now containing a secondary education component (Demsky 1994). Secondary education lending is still low compared with the 1960s and

BOX 12.1 MASSIVE EDUCATION REFORMS IN MEXICO'S POOR SOUTHERN STATES

Mexico has made strides in national education over the past few decades, and the country recently adopted aggressive reform policies to boost school achievement. Yet the poor states of the South, which lack the resources and administrative capability to exploit national advances, remain seriously behind the national average.

Now the Mexican government is pushing its reform agenda farther south. With help from a $412 million World Bank loan—one of the largest Bank social sector loans ever—and with more than $200 million of its own, Mexico is launching an ambitious primary education project in ten of the poorest southern states. Because of the project's targeted nature within the government's social compensatory program, project benefits will include a more equal distribution of economic opportunities among Mexican children, especially for underserved indigenous populations.

This Second Primary Education Project consists of three major components. First, a human resources development component will provide in-service training and assistance to upgrade the skills of primary school teachers, principals, and supervisors, emphasizing the role of principals and supervisors in providing pedagogical assistance to teachers in classroom teaching. Second, an educational material resources component will provide educational materials for both teachers and students; supply classroom library and reference books and promote their use; rehabilitate, replace, or build urgently needed educational facilities to replace inadequate schools and meet new enrollment demand; and design (in consultation with representatives of each indigenous community) and deliver bilingual textbooks and material for indigenous schools. Third, an institutional strengthening component will strengthen education management capacity at both central and state levels by providing management training for planning and policy analysis, installing project monitoring, evaluation, and information systems, conducting education studies to prepare future investments at the preschool and secondary education levels, and supporting project promotion and diffusion activities. This component will also improve the supervision system and strengthen the textbook and materials distribution system. Finally, the project will provide incentives for teachers to work in remote indigenous or hardship areas; absenteeism will be monitored directly by the local community and school council (World Bank 1994i).

1970s, when it accounted for more than half of all Bank education lending, but it is growing fast. Lending in recent years has reflected selective support for secondary education, particularly to improve equity for the poor and girls, to improve quality, and to increase external efficiency. A secondary education project in Colombia, for instance, includes a voucher program to enable poor students to attend private schools. The first free-standing female education project is for secondary education in Bangladesh.

Bank support for postsecondary education shows a mixed pattern. Lending for postsecondary vocational education and training has declined, consistent with Bank policy that this type of education is generally best provided on the job by employers (World Bank 1991c). Lending for teacher training remained roughly constant, at about 9 percent of total sector lending until fiscal 1990–94, when it fell to 7 percent and shifted away from preservice toward in-service training. During fiscal 1970–74, for instance, 49 percent of Bank projects contained preservice training components and 35 percent in-service components. For fiscal 1990–94 the comparable figures were 39 and 65 percent. Teacher training projects now support the development of training curricula, teacher training, and the development of instructional materials, whereas they were formerly mainly limited to the provision of teacher training facilities.

Lending for university and polytechnic-level higher education peaked at 36 percent of total lending in the mid-1980s; it has since fallen to about 26 percent. Originally directed mainly toward institutions that train professionals and technicians for the economy (such as agricultural universities), higher education projects increasingly support universities and institutions responsible for advanced scientific training and research. Several recent projects have also supported the improvement of links between industrial development and teaching and research in science and technology (Korea and China), the expansion of cost-sharing at public universities and the development of student loan and scholarship schemes (Kenya, Philippines, Tunisia, and Venezuela), and limitation of access to public universities (Côte d'Ivoire and Morocco). The bulk of postsecondary education projects in all categories have been in Africa and East Asia and the fewest in Latin America. Postsecondary education is expected to be an important component of future Bank education lending for the transition economies of Europe and Central Asia.

Regional Composition

Bank lending in the early 1980s was heavily concentrated in Africa, East Asia, and the Middle East. These regions' relative shares have declined as lending has expanded for primary education in South Asia and Latin America (figure 12.3). Absolute lending has increased in all regions, however. Lending is still relatively small in the Europe and Central Asia region. In the early years of Bank membership of the transition economies in this region, human resource projects tended to focus on social safety nets, labor markets, and health system rehabilitation.

FIGURE 12.3 WORLD BANK EDUCATION LENDING BY REGION, FISCAL 1964–94

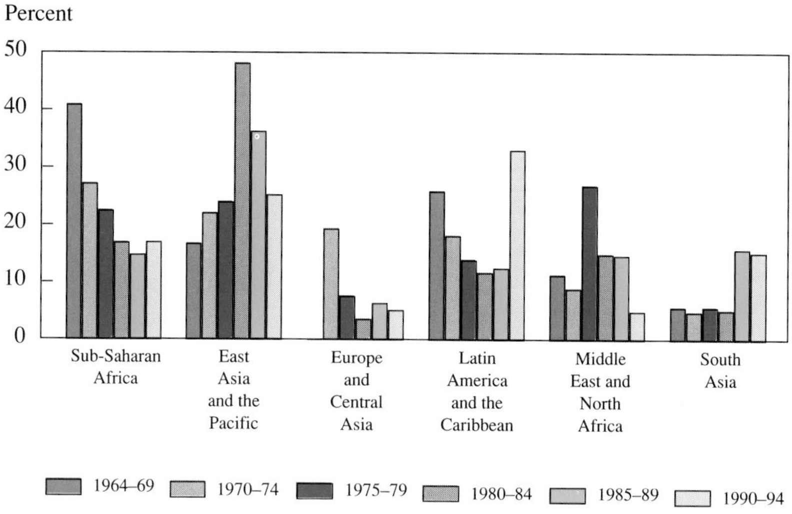

Percent

Source: World Bank data.

Girls' Education

Female education is receiving increased attention in Bank projects. Less than 15 percent of projects in the 1980s contained components to educate girls, but since 1990 this share has increased to 22 percent, and the trend is expected to continue. The regional distribution of female education components reflects regional differences in gender disparities. Lending has been concentrated on the Middle East (44 percent of all education projects address female education), South Asia (39 percent), and Africa (16 percent). Gender gaps in education are much less significant in East Asia, Europe and Central Asia, and Latin America, and hence there is little specific lending for girls in these regions.

Use of Bank Financing

In the early days of Bank lending for education and throughout the 1970s, more than half the funds lent by the Bank were used for civil works—to construct schools, colleges, and administration buildings. Since the mid-1980s this pro-

FIGURE 12.4   WORLD BANK EDUCATION LENDING BY EXPENDITURE CATEGORY, FISCAL 1964–94

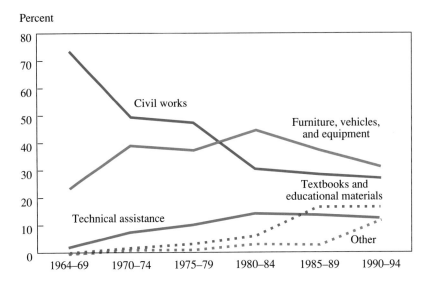

Source: World Bank data.

portion has fallen to about a quarter (figure 12.4). Bank loans increasingly finance inputs designed to improve the quality and the administration of education: textbooks, teacher training, laboratory equipment, learning assessments, examination systems, educational administration, technical assistance, and research. Despite this shift, Bank projects were always concerned with quality, even when most finance went to buildings. A few loans also finance the demand for education, through vouchers for the poor, as in Colombia; scholarships for girls, as in Bangladesh; and student loans, as in Venezuela. Overall, however, almost all Bank lending is for the supply of education services, as opposed to the demand.

Sectoral Approach

The use of Bank financing for inputs that improve quality as well as increase enrollments reflects a wider trend toward a sectoral approach to education. This trend is seen even more clearly in the integration of education within economic reform programs, in the emergence of education sectoral adjustment and sectoral investment loans, in the increasing inclusion of support for sectorwide reforms in specific investment loans, and in the Bank's continued attention to institution building.

Economic reform programs supported by the World Bank now routinely include measures to ensure that primary education is protected during fiscal adjustment. Recent structural adjustment loans to Guatemala, India, and Zimbabwe, for instance, support increases in public spending on primary education and other basic social services. There have been six education sector adjustment loans, the first in Morocco in fiscal 1986 and the others in Sub-Saharan Africa. These loans have tackled such sectoral issues as the allocation of public spending. In Guinea, for instance, a sector adjustment loan supports the redeployment of primary school teachers to underserved rural areas; in Kenya a loan supports the introduction of fees at public universities and the reversal of a trend toward ever-lower student-teacher ratios at primary and secondary schools. Thirty-nine sector investment loans have been made since 1979, mainly in Asia and Latin America, where institutions are relatively strong. These loans focus on institutional and policy reforms and use Bank finance to fund a share of an overall education public investment program. In the Philippines a sector loan supports a policy shift from the expansion of primary education toward a focus on its quality, efficiency, and equity. Procedures for efficient and equitable regional budget allocations in Colombia are supported by a sector investment loan. Specific education investment projects also include attention to sectorwide policies. The Fourth Education Project in Burkina Faso includes agreements to reduce spending on secondary and higher education subsidies by 10 percent annually.

Future Bank Support for Education

The volume of external assistance to education is impressive, but it is minor in comparison with spending on education by developing countries—by their governments and their people. A conservative estimate of public spending at 4 percent of GNP and private spending at 2 percent yields a total annual education expenditure of $270 billion for all low- and middle-income countries. All external finance together amounts to only 2.2 percent of this total, and World Bank financing to only 0.6 percent. This low share of total spending means that the Bank should concentrate on providing advice designed to help governments develop education policies suitable for the circumstances of their own countries.

Future operations will therefore adopt an even more explicit sectorwide policy focus to support changes in educational finance and management. This strategy may increase both the resources and the time needed to prepare projects, as key stakeholders must be involved in preparation. In increasingly decentralized contexts, these stakeholders will include not only central governments but also other levels of government, as well as communities, parents, teachers, and employers. The design of new operations will focus on the conditions needed to ensure successful implementation, which is the principal indicator of the Bank's development effectiveness. Effective implementation is especially important given the explosion in lending for education and the increased awareness of the importance of human resources.

Bank lending is already moving in the direction of the following six key areas of reform, described in part II of this report.

■ The Bank will continue to encourage its low- and middle-income country clients to give a higher priority to education and education reform (chapter 5) as an important complement to economic reform programs.

■ Education projects are taking more account of outcomes (chapter 6) and their relationship to educational inputs and processes at the institutional level. Accordingly, (a) more explicit use is being made of participatory methods in sector work and project design to ensure that all relevant clients are involved and that there is agreement on desired project outcomes and institutional-level conditions to produce the outcomes; (b) learning assessments are being employed to measure projects' impact on learning and on institutional environments; (c) more attention is being given to the collection of policy-related data; (d) monitoring and evaluation during and after project implementation are being improved; and (e) effectiveness indicators are being used more systematically. In addition, cost-benefit and cost-effectiveness analysis will be more systematically used both in sector work and in the identification, design, and appraisal of education projects.

■ The trend toward allocation of an increased share of lending to primary and lower-secondary education is expected to continue (chapter 7), with particular emphasis on the poorest countries that receive IDA funds and especially on Africa and South Asia. This emphasis will fit within the context of a sectoral approach that recognizes the importance of the various parts of the education system, the interdependencies among these parts, and the need to ensure that the focus, as well as the nature, of Bank assistance is based on a determination of where the Bank can be most useful in the particular circumstances of each country. Within basic education, quality is being more systematically encouraged, along with access and equity. In all regions increased private financing and private provision of higher education are being encouraged in the context of increased attention to fiscal sustainability.

▪ Equity is also receiving more systematic attention (chapter 8), to ensure a direct impact on poverty reduction. Increasing attention to girls' education is now accompanied by more attention to children from poor families and to disadvantaged groups, including ethnic minorities. Targeted early childhood development programs are becoming more important as a means of improving equity and later school performance.

▪ Projects support more household involvement in education (chapter 9), including participation in school management and (so far, only rarely) experimentation with school choice. Demand-side interventions, such as targeted scholarships for the poor, stipends for girls, and higher education loan schemes, are becoming more common. Since choice can run both equity and quality risks, experimentation requires more attention than in the past to the regulatory framework for education, including, in particular, quality-enhancing mechanisms, such as standard-setting, outcome monitoring, school inspection, and, at the higher level, accreditation.

▪ To enhance quality, projects are encouraging experimentation with the flexible and autonomous management of instructional resources (chapter 10) at the institutional level, complemented by attention to incentives for performance, such as examination systems, and to quality-enhancing mechanisms.

These six key areas of education system reform will be supported by future World Bank projects in the context of the guiding principles that the Bank adopted in 1994 to guide its operations: selectivity, partnership, client orientation, results orientation, cost effectiveness, and financial integrity (World Bank 1994h). For example:

Partnership will mean cooperation with other donors and agencies—particularly important as both multilateral and bilateral agencies increasingly focus their aid on the human resource sectors. Already the Latin America and the Caribbean region of the Bank is working in close partnership with the Inter-American Development Bank on social sector projects, as are the two Asia regions with the Asian Development Bank. The Human Development Department is working with UNESCO to improve the quality of international statistics on education. A possible difficulty in donor cooperation is the increasing adoption of a sectoral approach by many donors, not just the Bank. This makes cooperation on the policy framework imperative, placing new demands on many donors' capacity to provide analytical policy advice on the education system as a whole.

Client orientation is reflected in this report's focus on stakeholder involvement in educational reform. Several regions, particularly Africa, Latin America and the Caribbean, and South Asia, are enlarging their education presence in field offices to achieve such involvement. The Europe and Central Asia region has established a human resources "hub" in Hungary. In all regions there is increasing emphasis on the participation of potential beneficiaries in project design and implementation.

Results orientation in the education sector will mean even more attention to project outcomes. This will involve more intense efforts to help countries improve their education data; inclusion of more learning assessment components; more links between sector work and lending; more use of benefit-cost analysis in project identification, design, and appraisal; increased attention to monitoring and evaluation during and after project implementation; and renewed efforts to strengthen borrowers' educational administrations.

References

Abadzi, Helen. 1994. *What We Know about Adult Literacy: Is There Hope?* World Bank Discussion Paper 245. Washington, D.C.

Adams, Don, and Esther E. Gottlieb. 1993. *Education and Social Change in Korea.* New York: Garland.

Ahmed, Manzoor, Colette Chabbott, Arun Joshi, and Rohini Pande. 1993. *Primary Education for All: Learning from the BRAC Experience. A Case Study.* Project ABEL (Advancing Basic Education and Literacy). Washington, D.C.: Academy for Educational Development.

Ainsworth, Martha, Mead Over, and A. A. Rwegarulira. 1992. "Economic Impact of AIDS on Orphaned Children: What Does the Evidence Show?" Prepared for the Expert Meeting on Family and Development, Washington, D.C., July 16–17. National Academy of Sciences, Washington, D.C.

Albrecht, Douglas, and Adrian Ziderman. 1991. *Deferred Cost Recovery for Higher Education: Student Loan Programs in Developing Countries.* World Bank Discussion Paper 137. Washington, D.C.

Arrow, Kenneth J. 1993. "Excellence and Equity in Higher Education." *Education Economics* 1(1):5–12.

Associates in Rural Development. 1993. "Predicaments of Decentralization." *Forum for Advancing Basic Education and Literacy* 2(3):12–13.

Azariadis, Costas, and Allen Drazen, 1990. "Threshold Externalities in Economic Development." *Quarterly Journal of Economics* 105(2):501–26.

Barnett, W. S. 1992. "Benefits of Compensatory Preschool Education." *Journal of Human Resources* 27(2):279–312.

Barr, Nicholas. 1993. *The Economics of the Welfare State.* Stanford, Calif.: Stanford University Press.

Barro, R. J. 1991. "Economic Growth in a Cross-Section of Countries." *Quarterly Journal of Economics* 106(2):407–44.

Bartel, Ann P., and Frank R. Lichtenberg. 1987. "The Comparative Advantage of Educated Workers in Implementing New Technology." *Review of Economics and Statistics* 69(1):1–11.

Bashir, Sajitha. 1994. "Public versus Private in Primary Education: Comparisons of School Effectiveness and Costs in Tamil Nadu." Ph.D. dissertation. University of London.

Becker, Gary S. 1964. *Human Capital: A Theoretical and Empirical Analysis, with Special Reference to Education*. General Series 30. New York: Columbia University Press.

Benavot, Aaron, and David Kamens. 1989. "The Curricular Content of Primary Education in Developing Countries." Policy Research Working Paper 237. World Bank, Education and Social Policy Department, Washington, D.C.

Berg, Alan. 1987. *Malnutrition: What Can Be Done? Lessons from World Bank Experience*. Baltimore, Md.: Johns Hopkins University Press.

Bhowon, Rajayswar, and V. Chinapah. 1993. "Reform of Basic Education in Mauritius: The Process of Information Gathering, Consultation and Decision-Making." In David W. Chapman and Lars O. Mälck, eds., *Information Systems in Educational Planning: From Data to Action*. Paris: UNESCO, International Institute for Educational Planning.

Blackburn, M. L. 1990. "What Can Explain the Increase in Earnings Inequality among Males?" *Industrial Relations* 29(3):441–56.

Blackburn, M. L., D. E. Bloom, and R. B. Freeman. 1990. "The Declining Economic Position of Less Skilled American Males." In Gary T. Burtless, ed., *A Future of Lousy Jobs? The Changing Structure of U.S. Wages*. Washington, D.C.: Brookings Institution.

Blaug, Mark. 1976. "The Empirical Status of Human Capital Theory: A Slightly Jaundiced Survey." *Journal of Economic Literature* 14:827–55.

Boissière, Maurice, J. B. Knight, and R. H. Sabot. 1985. "Earnings, Schooling, Ability, and Cognitive Skills." *American Economic Review* 75 (December):1016–30.

Bound, John, and George Johnson. 1992. "Changes in the Structure of Wages during the 1980s: An Evaluation of Alternative Explanations." *American Economic Review* 82(3):371–92.

Bowman, Mary Jean, and C. Arnold Anderson. 1963. "Concerning the Role of Education in Development." In Clifford Geertz, ed., *Old Societies and New States: The Quest for Modernity in Asia and Africa*. New York: Free Press of Glencoe.

Bray, Mark. 1987. School Clusters in the Third World: Making Them Work. Paris: UNESCO-UNICEF Cooperative Program.

———. 1990. "The Economics of Multiple-Shift Schooling: Research Evidence and Research Gaps." *International Journal of Educational Development* 10(2/3):181–87.

Bray, Mark, with Kevin Lilli. 1988. *Community Financing of Education: Issues and Policy Implications in Less Developed Countries*. New York: Pergamon Press.

Bridge, Gary R., Charles M. Judd, and Peter R. Moock. 1979. *The Determinants of Educational Outcomes: The Impact of Families, Peers, Teachers and Schools*. Cambridge, Mass.: Ballinger.

Brookover, Wilbur B., and L. W. Lezotte. 1979. *Changes in School Characteristics Coincident with Changes in Student Achievement*. Institute for Research on Teaching Occasional Paper 17. East Lansing, Mich.: Michigan State University Press.

Brubaker, H., and R. Partine. 1986. "Implementing Effective Schools Research: The Audit Process. High School Observations." Paper presented at conference of American Educational Research Association, San Francisco, April 16–20.

Bryant, D. M., and C. T. Ramey. 1987. "An Analysis of the Effectiveness of Early Intervention Programs for Environmentally At-Risk Children." In Michael J. Guralnick and Forrest C. Bennett, eds., *The Effectiveness of Early Intervention for At-Risk and Handicapped Children.* Orlando, Fla.: Academic Press.

Bundy, D. A. P. and others. 1990. "Control of Geohelminths by Delivery of Targeted Chemotherapy through Schools." *Transactions of the Royal Society of Tropical Medicine and Hygiene* 84:115–20.

Butt, Abdul Rauf, and Mohammed Amjad Sheikh. 1988. "An Analysis of the Gap between Demand for and Supply of Higher Education in Pakistan." *Pakistan Economic and Social Review* 26(1):41–56.

Caldwell, J. C. 1979. "Education as a Factor in Mortality Decline: An Examination of Nigerian Data." *Population Studies* 33(3):395–413.

Carter, C., and J. Klotz. 1990. "What Principals Must Know Before Assuming the Role of Instructional Leader." *NASSP Bulletin* 74(525):36–41.

Chaturvedi, S., B. C. Srivastava, J. V. Singh, and M. Prasad. 1987. "Impact of Six Years Exposure to ICDS Scheme on Psycho-Social Development." *Indian Pediatrics* 24(2):153–60.

Chernichovsky, Dov. 1985. "Socioeconomic and Demographic Aspects of School Enrollment and Attendance in Rural Botswana." *Economic Development and Cultural Change* 32:319–32.

Chiswick, Barry R. 1991. "Speaking, Reading and Earnings among Low-Skilled Immigrants." *Journal of Labor Economics* 9(2):149–70.

Chiswick, Barry R., and Paul W. Miller. 1995. "The Endogeneity between Language and Earnings: International Analyses." *Journal of Labor Economics* 13(2):246–88.

Chowdhury, Kowar. 1993. "Women's Education: Barriers and Solutions." World Bank, Education and Social Policy Department, Washington, D.C.

Chubb, John, and Terry M. Moe. 1990. *Politics, Markets and America's Schools.* Washington, D.C.: Brookings Institution.

Chutikul, Sirilaksana. 1986. *The Effect of Tuition Fee Increases on the Demand for Higher Education: A Case Study of a Higher Education Institution in Thailand.* Sussex, U.K.: University of Sussex.

Cleland, John, and Christopher Wilson. 1987. "Demand Theories of the Fertility Transition: An Iconoclastic View." *Population Studies* 41:5–30.

Colbert, Vicky, C. Chiappe, and J. Arboleda. 1993. "The New School Program: More and Better Primary Education for Children in Colombia." In Henry M. Levin and Marlaine E. Lockheed, eds., *Effective Schools In Developing Countries.* London: Falmer Press.

Colclough, Christopher. 1990. "Raising Additional Resources for Education in Developing Countries: Are Graduate Payroll Taxes Superior to Student Loans?" *International Journal of Educational Development* 10(2/3):169–80.

Colletta, Nat J., and Gillian Perkins. 1995. "Participation in Education." Participation Series Paper. World Bank, Environment Department, Washington, D.C.

Colletta, Nat J., and Margaret Sutton. 1989. "Achieving and Sustaining Universal Primary Education: International Experience Relevant to India." Policy Research Working Paper 166. World Bank, Population and Human Resources Department, Washington, D.C.

Commonwealth Secretariat. 1994. "The Changing Role of the State in Education: Politics and Partnerships. An Overview of Country Papers." Agenda Item 2, Twelfth Conference of Commonwealth Education Ministers, Islamabad, Pakistan. London.

Cox-Edwards, Alejandra. 1994. "Chile: Strategy for Rural Areas—Enhancing Agricultural Competitiveness and Alleviating Rural Poverty." In "Rural Labor Markets." Report 12776-Chile. World Bank, Washington, D.C.

Dalin, Per, in cooperation with Tekle Ayano, Anbesu Biazen, Mumtaz Jahan, Matthew Miles and Carlos Rojas. 1992. *How Schools Improve*. Oslo: International Movements toward Educational Change (IMTEC).

David, J. L., and S. M. Peterson. 1984. *Can Schools Improve Themselves? A Study of School-Based Improvement Programs*. San Francisco: Bay Area Research Group.

Davis, S. J. 1992. "Cross-Country Patterns of Change in Relative Wages." *NBER Macroeconomics Annual 1992*. Cambridge, Mass.: MIT Press.

Demsky, Terry. 1994. "World Bank Lending for Secondary Education: A General Operational Review." World Bank, Education and Social Policy Department, Washington, D.C.

Denison, Edward F. 1967. *Why Growth Rates Differ: Post-War Experience in Nine Western Countries*. Washington, D.C.: Brookings Institution.

Derfler, Frank. 1992. *PC Guide to Connectivity*. Emeryville, Calif.: Ziff-Davis.

Dhanani, S. 1993. "Indonesian Manufacturing Employment and Training." Vol. 1, "Major Findings of the 1992 West Java Enterprise Survey." Technical Report 2. BAPPENAS, Bureau of Manpower, Regional Manpower Planning and Training Project (World Bank Professional Human Resources Development Loan 3134-ID), Jakarta, Indonesia.

Donors to African Education. 1994. *A Statistical Profile of Education in Sub-Saharan Africa in the 1980s*. Paris.

Dutcher, Nadine, in collaboration with G. R. Tucker. 1994. "The Use of First and Second Languages in Education: A Review of Educational Experience." World Bank, East Asia and the Pacific Region, Country Department III, Washington, D.C.

Easterlin, Richard A. 1981. "Why Isn't the Whole World Developed?" *Journal of Economic History* 41(1):1–15.

Easterly, William, and Stanley Fischer. 1994. "What We Can Learn from the Soviet Collapse." *Finance and Development* 31(4): 2–5.

Eckstein, Max A., and Harold J. Noah. 1993. *Secondary School Examinations: International Perspectives on Policies and Practices*. New Haven, Conn.: Yale University Press.

Eisemon, Thomas Owen. 1988. *Benefiting from Basic Education, School Quality, and Functional Literacy in Kenya*. Comparative and International Education Series 2. Oxford: Pergamon Press.

————. 1989. "What Language Should be Used for Teaching? Language Policy and School Reform in Burundi." *Journal of Multilingual and Multicultural Development* 10(6):473–97.

Eisemon, Thomas Owen, and John Schwille. 1991. "Primary Schooling in Burundi and Kenya: Preparation for Secondary Education or for Self-Employment?" *Elementary School Journal* 92(1):23–39.

Eisemon, Thomas Owen, J. Ratzlaff, and V. L. Patel. 1992. "Reading Instructions for Using Commercial Medicines." *Annals of the American Academy of Political and Social Science* 520:76–90.

Eisemon, Thomas Owen, John Schwille, and Robert Prouty. 1989. "Empirical Results and Conventional Wisdom: Strategies for Increasing Primary School Effectiveness in Burundi." Draft report, BRIDGES Project. Harvard Institute for International Development, Cambridge, Mass.

————. 1992. "Can Schooling Make a Better Farmer? Outcomes of Agricultural Education in Burundi." In G. G. Mades, ed., *Primary School Agriculture in Sub-Saharan Africa*. Eschborn: Deutsche Gesellschaft für Technische Zusammenarbeit.

Eisemon, Thomas Owen, I. Mihailescu, L. Vlasceanu, C. Davis, J. Sheehan, and C. Zamfir. Forthcoming. "Higher Education Reform in Romania." *Higher Education*.

Frederick, J. M. 1987. *Measuring School Effectiveness: Guidelines for Educational Practitioners*. ERIC Clearing House on Test Measurement and Evaluation, Educational Testing Services, Princeton, N.J.

Fuller, Bruce, and P. Clarke. 1994. "Raising School Effects While Ignoring Culture? Local Conditions and the Influence of Classroom Tools, Rules and Pedagogy." *Review of Educational Research* 64(1):119–57.

Fuller, Bruce, H. Hua, and C. W. Snyder. 1994. "When Girls Learn More than Boys: The Influence of Time in School and Pedagogy in Botswana." *Comparative Education Review* 38(3):347–77.

GAO (U.S. General Accounting Office). 1994. *Education Reform: School-Based Management Results in Changes in Instruction and Budgeting*. Washington, D.C.

Gertler, Paul, and Paul Glewwe. 1989. *The Willingness to Pay for Education in Developing Countries: Evidence from Rural Peru*. Living Standards Measurement Study Working Paper 54. Washington, D.C.: World Bank.

Gibbs, Greg K. 1989. *Effective Schools Research: The Principal as Instructional Leader*. Washington, D.C.: U.S. Department of Education.

Gill, Indermit, and Michelle Riboud. 1993. "Productivity Growth and Wage Structures in Mexico and the U.S.: Surmising the Employment Effects of the NAFTA." World Bank, Latin America and the Caribbean Region, Country Department II, Washington, D.C.

González-Suárez, Mirta. 1987. "Barriers to Female Achievement: Sex Stereotypes in Textbooks." Paper presented to the Comparative and International Education Society, Washington, D.C.

Gould, David M., and Roy J. Ruffin. 1993. "What Determines Economic Growth?" *Economic Review, Federal Reserve of Dallas* (2d quarter).

Greaney, Vincent, and Thomas Kellaghan. 1995. *Equity Issues in Public Examinations in Developing Countries.* World Bank Technical Paper 272. Washington, D.C.

Griffin, Peter, and Alejandra Cox-Edwards. 1993. "Rates of Return to Education in Brazil: Do Labor Market Conditions Matter?" *Economics of Education Review* 12(3):245–57.

Haddad, Wadi D. 1994. *The Dynamics of Education Policymaking: Case Studies of Burkina Faso, Jordan, Peru and Thailand.* EDI Development Policy Case Studies Series, Analytical Case Studies 10. Washington, D.C.: World Bank.

Haddad, Wadi D., Martin Carnoy, Rosemary Rinaldi, and Omporn Regel. 1990. *Education and Development: Evidence for New Priorities.* World Bank Discussion Paper 95. Washington, D.C.

Hallinger, Phillip. 1989. "Developing Instructional Leadership Teams in High Schools." In Bert Creemers, Tony Peters, and David Reynolds, eds., *School Effectiveness and School Improvement: Proceedings of the Second International Congress.* Amsterdam: Swets and Zeitlinger.

Halpern, Robert. 1986. "Effects of Early Childhood Intervention on Primary School Progress in Latin America." *Comparative Education Review* 30(2):193–215.

Hannaway, Jane. 1991. "The Organization and Management of Public and Catholic Schools: Looking Inside the `Black Box.'" *International Journal of Educational Research* 16:463–81.

———. 1993. "Decentralization in Two Districts: Challenging the Standard Paradigm." In Jane Hannaway and M. Carnoy, eds., *Decentralization and School Improvement: Can We Fulfill the Promise?* San Francisco: Jossey-Bass.

Hanushek, Eric A. 1994. "Outcomes, Costs and Incentives in Schools." Paper prepared for the conference on Improving the Performance of America's Schools: Economic Choices. U.S. National Research Council, Washington, D.C..

Harbison, Ralph W., and Eric A. Hanushek. 1992. *Educational Performance of the Poor: Lessons from Rural Northeast Brazil.* New York: Oxford University Press.

Herz, Barbara, K. Subbarao, Masooma Habib, and Laura Raney. 1991. *Letting Girls Learn: Promising Approaches in Primary and Secondary Education.* World Bank Discussion Paper 133. Washington, D.C.

Heyneman, Stephen P. 1994. "Education in the Europe and Central Asia Region: Policies of Adjustment and Excellence." Internal Discussion Paper 145. World Bank, Europe and Central Asia Region, Washington, D.C.

Heyneman, Stephen P., Joseph P. Farrell, and Manuel A. Sepulveda-Stuardo. 1978. *Textbooks and Achievement: What We Know.* World Bank Staff Working Paper 298. Washington, D.C.

Himmel, Erika. 1995. *Case Study of National Assessment in Chile.*" EDI Development Policy Case Series. World Bank, Washington, D.C.

Hobcraft, John. 1993. "Women's Education, Child Welfare, and Child Survival: A Review of the Evidence." *Health Transition Review* 3(2):159–75.

Holsinger, Donald. 1994. "Thailand: Proposed Secondary Education and Teacher Training Project." World Bank, Education and Social Policy Department, Washington, D.C.

Holsinger, Donald, and David Baker. 1993. "The Size and Structure of Secondary Education in Developing Countries." ESP Discussion Paper 7. World Bank, Education and Social Policy Department, Washington, D.C.

Hyde, Karin. 1989. "Improving Women's Education in Sub-Saharan Africa: A Review of the Literature." PHREE Background Paper Series 15. World Bank, Education and Social Policy Department, Washington, D.C.

IEA (International Association for the Evaluation of Educational Achievement). 1994. *Indicators of Between-School Differences in Reading Achievement.* Prepared by Andres Schleicher and Jean Yip. The Hague.

ILO (International Labour Office). 1992. *World Labor Report.* Geneva.

Jain, Balbir. 1991. "Returns to Education: Further Analysis of Cross-Country Data." *Economics of Education Review* 10(3):253–58.

Jarousse, J. P., and Alain Mingat. 1993. *Options for Accelerated Development of Primary Education in the Sahel.* IREDU-CNRS, Université de Bourgogne, France.

Jimenez, Emmanuel. 1987. *Pricing Policy in the Social Sectors: Cost Recovery for Education and Health in Developing Countries.* Baltimore, Md.: Johns Hopkins University Press.

Joyce, Bruce R. 1991. "The Doors to School Improvement." *Educational Leadership* 48(8):59–62.

Joyce, Bruce R., and Beverly Showers. 1985. *Power in Staff Development through Research on Training.* Alexandria, Va.: Association for Supervision and Curriculum Development.

———. 1987. "Low-Cost Arrangements for Peer-Coaching." *Educational Leadership* 45(2):22–24.

———. 1988. *Student Achievement Through Staff Development.* New York: Longman.

Joyce, Bruce R., Richard H. Hersh, and Michael McKibbin. 1983. *The Structure of School Improvement.* New York: Longman.

Kagitcibasi, Cigdem, D. Sunar, and S. Bekman. 1987. "Comprehensive Preschool Education Project: Final Report." International Development Research Centre, Ottawa.

Kellaghan, Thomas, and Vincent Greaney. 1992. *Using Examinations to Improve Education: A Study of Fourteen African Countries.* World Bank Technical Paper 165. Washington, D.C.

Kelly, Michael J., Eileen B. Nkwanga, L. Henry Kaluba, Paul P. W. Achola, and K. Nilsson. 1986. "The Provision of Education for All: Final Report of the Education Reform Implementation Project." University of Zambia, School of Education, Lusaka.

Knight, John B., and Richard H. Sabot. 1990. *Education, Productivity, and Inequality: The East African Natural Experiment.* New York: Oxford University Press.

Korea, Ministry of Education. 1992. *Education in Korea: 1991–1992.* National Institute of Educational Research and Training, Seoul.

Laporte, Bruno, and Julian Schweitzer. 1994. "Education and Training." In Nicholas Barr, ed., *Labor Markets and Social Policy in Central and Eastern Europe: The Transition and Beyond.* New York: Oxford University Press.

Larach, Linda, and Marlaine E. Lockheed. 1992. "World Bank Lending for Educational Testing." PHREE Background Paper 91/62R. World Bank, Education and Social Policy Department, Washington, D.C.

Lau, Lawrence J., Dean T. Jamison, and Frederic F. Louat. 1991. "Education and Productivity in Developing Countries: An Aggregate Production Function Approach." Policy Research Working Paper 612. World Bank, Development Economics and Population and Human Resources Department, Washington, D.C.

Lau, Lawrence J., Dean T. Jamison, S. C. Liu, and S. Rivkin. 1993. "Education and Economic Growth: Some Cross-Sectional Evidence from Brazil." *Journal of Development Economics* 41:45–70.

Lee, Valerie E., and Marlaine E. Lockheed. 1990. "The Effects of Single-Sex Schooling on Student Achievement in Attitudes in Nigeria." *Comparative Education Review* 34(2):209–32.

Leo-Rhynie, E. 1981. *Report on The Shift System in Jamaican Schools.* University of the West Indies, School of Education, Mona, Jamaica.

Levin, Henry M., and Marlaine E. Lockheed, eds.. *Effective Schools In Developing Countries.* London: Falmer Press.

Levine, Daniel U. 1990. "Update on Effective Schools: Findings and Implications from Research and Practice." *Journal of Negro Education* 59(4):577–84.

Levine, Daniel U., and Lawrence W. Lezotte. 1990. "Unusually Effective Schools: A Review and Analysis of Research and Practice." National Center for Effective Schools Research and Development, Madison, Wis.

LeVine, Robert, S. E. Levine, A. Richman, F. M. Tapia Uribe, C. S. Correa, and P. M. Miller. 1991. "Women's Schooling and Child Care in the Demographic Transition: A Mexican Case Study." *Population and Development Review* 17(3):459–96.

Levinger, Beryl. 1992. "Nutrition, Health and Learning: Current Trends and Issues." School Nutrition and Health Network Monograph Series 1. Education Development Center, Newton, Mass.

Lezotte, L. W., and B. A. Bancroft. 1985. "Growing Use of the Effective School Model." *Educational Leadership* 42(6):23–27.

Lezotte, L. W., and others. 1980. *School Learning Climate and Academic Achievement: A Social Systems Approach to Increase Student Learning.* Site-Specific Technical Assistance Center, Florida State University Foundation, Tallahassee, Fla.

Lindenbaum, Shirley, Manisha Chakraborty, and Mohammed Elias. 1989. "The Influence of Maternal Education on Infant and Child Mortality in Bangladesh." In John C. Caldwell and Gigi Santow, eds., *Selected Readings in the Cultural, Social and Behavioral Determinants of Health.* Health Transition Series 1. Canberra: Highland Press.

Lindert, Paul H. 1976. "Child Costs and Economic Development." In R. A. Easterlin, ed., *Population and Economic Change in Developing Countries.* Chicago: University of Chicago Press.

Lockheed, Marlaine E., and Eric Hanushek. 1988. "Improving Educational Efficiency in Developing Countries: What Do We Know?" *Compare* 18(1):21–38.

Lockheed, Marlaine E., and Emmanuel Jimenez. 1994. "Public and Private Secondary Schools in Developing Countries." Human Resources Development and Operations Policy Working Paper 43. World Bank, Washington, D.C.

Lockheed, Marlaine E., Josefina Fonacier, and Leonard J. Bianchi. 1989. "Effective Primary Level Science Teaching in the Philippines." Policy Research Working Paper 208. World Bank, Education and Social Policy Department, Washington, D.C.

Lockheed, Marlaine E., Dean T. Jamison, and Lawrence Lau. 1980. "Farmer Education and Farm Efficiency: A Survey." *Economic Development and Cultural Change* 29 (October):37–76.

Lockheed, Marlaine E., John Middleton, and Greta S. Nettleton, eds. 1991. "Education Technology: Sustainable and Effective Use." PHREE Background Paper 91/32. World Bank, Education and Social Policy Department, Washington, D.C.

Lockheed, Marlaine E., Adriaan M. Verspoor, and others. 1991. *Improving Primary Education in Developing Countries*. New York: Oxford University Press.

Loh, Eng Seng. 1992. "Technological Changes, Training, and the Inter-Industry Wage Structure." *Quarterly Review of Economics and Finance* 32(4):26–44.

Lombard, Avima. 1994. *Success Begins at Home: The Past, Present and Future of the Home Instruction Program for Preschool Youngsters*. Dushkin, Conn.: Guilford.

Loury, G. 1977. "A Dynamic Theory of Racial Income Differences." In P. A. Wallace and A. M. LaMond, eds., *Women, Minorities, and Employment Discrimination*. New York: Macmillan.

———. 1987. "Why Should We Care about Group Inequality?" *Social Philosophy and Policy* 5:249–71.

Lucas, R. E. 1988. "On the Mechanics of Economic Development." *Journal of Monetary Economics* 22:3–22.

Lundberg, Ingvar, and Pirjo Linnakyla. 1992. *Teaching Reading Around the World*. The Hague: International Association for the Evaluation of Educational Achievement.

Madaus, G. F., and V. Greaney. 1985. "The Irish Experience in Competency Education: Implications for American Education." *American Journal of Education* 93:268–94.

Martin, C. L., and G. Levy. 1994. "Gender Roles and Preschool Education." *International Encyclopedia of Education,* vol. 4. 2d ed. New York: Pergamon Press.

Mason, Andrew David. 1994. "Schooling Decisions, Basic Education and the Poor in Rural Java." Ph.D. dissertation. Stanford University, Food Research Institute, Stanford, Calif.

McKnight, Allan. 1971. *Scientists Abroad; A Study of the International Movement of Persons in Science and Technology*. Paris: UNESCO.

McMahon, Walter W., and Boediono. 1992. "Market Signals and Labor Market Analysis: A New View of Manpower Supplies and Demands." In Walter W. McMahon and Boediono, eds., *Education and the Economy*. Jakarta: USAID.

McMahon, Walter W., and Jung, H. J. 1989. "Vocational and Technical Education in Indonesia: Theoretical Analysis and Evidence on Rates of Return." Faculty Working Paper 89-1582. University of Illinois, College of Commerce and Business Administration, Urbana-Champaign, Ill..

McNamara, Robert S. 1992. "The Post-Cold War World: Implications for Military Expenditure in the Developing Countries." In *Proceedings of the Annual Conference on Development Economics 1991*. Washington, D.C.: World Bank.

Middleton, John, Adrian Ziderman, and Arvil Van Adams. 1993. *Skills for Productivity: Vocational Education and Training in Developing Countries*. New York: Oxford University Press.

Mincer, Jacob. 1989. "Human Capital and the Labor Market: A Review of Current Research." *Educational Researcher* (May):27–34.

Mingat, Alain, and Jee-Peng Tan. 1985. "On Equity in Education Again: An International Comparison." *Journal of Human Resources* 20:298–308.

———. 1994. "International Perspectives on Education: Some Ideas for Data Analysis." World Bank, Education and Social Policy Department, Washington, D.C.

Mittler, Peter. 1992. "International Visions of Excellence for Children with Disabilities." *International Journal of Disability, Development and Education* 39(2):115–26.

Mittler, Peter, R. Brouillette, and D. Harris, eds. 1993. *World Year Book of Education.* London: Kegan Paul.

Moock, Peter. 1994. "Education and Agricultural Productivity." *International Encyclopedia of Education* 1:244–54. Oxford: Pergamon Press.

Moock, Peter, Philip Musgrove, and Morton Stelcner. 1990. *Education and Earnings in Peru's Informal Nonfarm Family Enterprises.* Living Standards Measurement Study Working Paper 64. Washington, D.C.: World Bank.

Murnane, Richard J., John B. Willett, and Frank Levy. 1993. *The Growing Importance of Cognitive Skills in Wage Determination.* Harvard University, Graduate School of Education and Massachusetts Institute of Technology, Department of Urban Studies and Planning, Cambridge, Mass.

Myers, Robert. 1992. *The Twelve Who Survive: Strengthening Programmes of Early Childhood Development in the Third World.* London: Routledge.

Myers, Robert, and others. 1985. "Pre-School Education as a Catalyst for Community Development: An Evaluation." USAID, Lima.

NCERT (National Council for Education Research and Training). 1994. *Minimum Learning Continuum.* New Delhi.

National Technological University. 1994. "The National Technological University: Background." Fort Collins, Colo.

Nielsen, H. Dean, and M. T. Tatto. 1991. *The Cost Effectiveness of Distance Education for Teacher Training.* BRIDGES Research Report 9. Harvard Institute for International Development, Cambridge, Mass.

Nitsaisook, Malee, and Lorin W. Anderson. 1989. "An Experimental Investigation of the Effectiveness of In-Service Teacher Education in Thailand." *Teacher and Training Education* 5(4):287–302.

Noss, Andrew. 1991. "Education and Adjustment: A Review of the Literature." Policy Research Working Paper 701. World Bank, Education and Social Policy Department, Washington, D.C.

OECD (Organisation for Economic Co-operation and Development). 1993. *Education at a Glance: OECD Indicators.* Paris: OECD, Centre for Educational Research and Innovation.

———. 1994a. *The Markets for Learning and Educational Services.* Paris: OECD, Centre for Educational Research and Innovation.

———. 1994b. *School: A Matter of Choice.* Paris: OECD, Centre for Educational Research and Innovation.

Orazem, Peter F., and Milan Vodopivec. 1994. "Winners and Losers in Transition: Returns to Education, Experience, and Gender in Slovenia." Policy Research Working Paper 1342. World Bank, Policy Research Department, Washington, D.C.

Patrinos, Harry A. 1994. "Education and Earnings Differentials During the 1980s." World Bank, Education and Social Policy Department, Washington, D.C.

Patrinos, Harry A., and George Psacharopoulos. 1995. "Educational Performance and Child Labor in Paraguay." *International Journal of Educational Development* 15(1):47–60.

Patrinos, Harry A., Eduardo Velez, and George Psacharopoulos. 1994. "Language, Education and Earnings in Asuncion, Paraguay." *Journal of Developing Areas* 29(1):57–68.

Pollitt, Ernesto. 1990. *Malnutrition and Infection in the Classroom.* Paris: UNESCO.

Postlethwaite, T. N., and Kenneth Ross. 1992. *Effective Schools in Reading: Implications for Educational Planners.* The Hague: International Association for the Evaluation of Educational Achievement.

Prawda, Juan. 1993. "Educational Decentralization in Latin America: Lessons Learned." *International Journal of Educational Development* 13:253–64.

Psacharopoulos, George. 1987. "To Vocationalize or Not to Vocationalize? That Is the Curriculum Question." *International Journal of Education Development* 33(2):187–211.

———. 1989. "Time Trends of the Returns to Education: Cross-National Evidence." *Economics of Education Review* 8(3):225–31.

———. 1994. "Returns to Investment in Education: A Global Update." *World Development* 22(9):1325–43.

Psacharopoulos, George, and Harry A. Patrinos. 1994. *Indigenous People and Poverty in Latin America: An Empirical Analysis.* A World Bank Regional and Sectoral Study. Washington, D.C.

Psacharopoulos, George, and Zafiris Tzannatos. 1992. *Case Studies on Women's Employment and Pay in Latin America.* A World Bank Regional and Sectoral Study, Washington, D.C.

Psacharopoulos, George, and Eduardo Velez. 1993. "Educational Quality and Labor Market Outcomes: Evidence from Bogota, Colombia." *Sociology of Education* 66:130–45.

Psacharopoulos, George, and Maureen Woodhall. 1985. *Education for Development: An Analysis of Investment Choices.* New York: Oxford University Press.

Psacharopoulos, George, Carlos Rojas, and Eduardo Velez. 1993. "Achievement Evaluation of Colombia's Escuela Nueva: Is Multigrade the Answer?" *Comparative Education Review* 37(3):263–76.

Psacharopoulos, George, Eduardo Velez, and Harry Anthony Patrinos. 1994. "Education and Earnings in Paraguay." *Economics of Education Review* 13(4):321–27.

Purkey, Stewart C., and Marshall S. Smith. 1983. "Effective Schools: A Review." *Elementary School Journal* 83(4):427–52.

Puryear, Jeffrey. 1995. "International Education Statistics and Research: Status and Problems." *International Journal of Educational Development* 15(1):79–91.

Raudenbush, Stephen W., C. Bhumirat, and M. Kamali. 1989. *Predictors and Conse-quences of Teachers' Knowledge in Thailand.* BRIDGES Project. Harvard Institute for International Development, Cambridge, Mass.

Richards, M., and J. Richards. 1990. *Languages and Communities Encompassed by Guatemala's National Bilingual Education Program.* USAID in conjunction with the Ministerio de Educación de Guatemala.

Rodríguez, Germán, and John Cleland. 1980. "Socio-Economic Determinants of Mari-tal Fertility in Twenty Countries: A Multivariate Analysis." *World Fertility Survey Conference 1980: Record of Proceedings.* Vol. 2. London: World Fertility Survey.

Romer, P. M. 1986. "Increasing Returns and Long-Run Growth." *Journal of Political Economy* 94:1002–37.

Rosenzweig, Mark R. 1995. "Why Are There Returns to Schooling?" *American Eco-nomic Review* 85(2):153–58.

Ross, Kenneth N., and Lars Mählck. 1990. *Planning the Quality of Education: The Collection and Use of Data for Informed Decision-Making.* Paris: UNESCO.

Ross, Kenneth, and T. N. Postlethwaite. 1989. *Indonesia: Quality of Basic Education.* Jakarta: Ministry of Education and Culture.

Sadlak, Jan. 1993. "Legacy and Change: Higher Education and the Restoration of Academic Work in Romania." *Technology in Society* 15(1):75–100.

Salmi, Jamil. 1991. "Perspectives on the Financing of Higher Education." PHREE Back-ground Paper 91/45. World Bank, Education and Social Policy Department, Wash-ington, D.C.

Sapsford, David, and Zafiris Tzannatos. 1993. *The Economics of the Labour Market.* Basingstoke, U.K.: Macmillan.

Sathar, Zeba A., and Cynthia B. Lloyd. 1993. *Who Gets Primary Schooling in Pakistan? Inequalities among and within Families.* Working Paper 52. New York: Popula-tion Council.

Schaeffer, E. S. 1987. "Parental Modernity and Child Academic Competence: Toward a Theory of Individual and Societal Development." *Early Childhood Development and Care* 27:373–89.

Scheerens, Jaap, and Bert Creemers. 1989. "Towards a More Comprehensive Conceptualization of School Effectiveness." In Bert Creemers, T. Peters, and D. Reynolds, eds., *School Effectiveness and School Improvement.* Amsterdam: Swets and Zeitlinger.

Schultz, T. Paul. 1993. "Investments in Schooling and Health of Women and Men: Quantities and Return." *Journal of Human Resources* 28(4):694–734.

———. 1994. "Integrated Approaches to Human Resource Development." World Bank, Human Resources Development and Operations Policy Vice-Presidency, Wash-ington, D.C.

Schultz, Theodore W. 1961. "Education and Economic Growth." In N. B. Henry, ed., *Social Forces Influencing American Education.* Chicago: University of Chicago Press.

———. 1975. "The Value of the Ability to Deal with Disequilibria." *Journal of Eco-nomic Literature* 13(3):827–46.

————. 1982. *Investing in People: The Economics of Population Quality.* Berkeley: University of California Press.

Schweinhart, L. J., and J. J. Koshel. 1986. *Policy Options for Preschool Programs.* Ypsilanti, Mich.: High/Scope Education Research Foundation.

Selowsky, Marcelo. 1979. *Who Benefits from Government Expenditures? A Case Study of Colombia.* New York: Oxford University Press.

————. 1980. "Preschool Age Investment in Human Capital." In John Simmons, ed., *The Education Dilemma.* Oxford: Pergamon Press.

————. 1983. "Nutrition, Health and Education: The Economic Significance of Complementarities at Early Ages." In Paul Streeten and Harry Maier, eds., *Concepts, Measurement, and Long-Run Perspective.* Vol 2. of *Human Resources, Employment, and Development: Proceedings of the Sixth World Congress of the International Economic Association Held in Mexico City, 1980.* New York: St. Martin's Press.

Shaeffer, Sheldon. 1993. *The Impact of HIV/AIDS on Education Systems. Educational Horizons* 71(4):171–74.

Shavelson, Richard J. 1981. *Conclusions and Policy Implications.* Vol. 7 of *A Study of Alternatives in American Education.* Santa Monica, Calif.: Rand.

Singh, Janardan P. 1990. "Analysis of Project Costs in Sub-Saharan Africa in Selected Sectors." In *Economic and Sectoral Policy Issues.* World Bank Long-Term Perspective Study of Sub-Saharan Africa Background Paper 2. Washington, D.C.

Sivin-Kachala, Jay, and Ellen R. Bialo. 1994. *Report on the Effectiveness of Technology in Schools, 1990–94.* Interactive Educational Systems Design, New York.

Smith, Wilma F., and Richard L. Andrews. 1989. *Instructional Leadership: How Principals Make a Difference.* Alexandria, Va.: Association for Supervision and Curriculum Development.

Smylie, M. A. 1994. "Redesigning Teachers' Work: Connections to the Classroom." In L. Darling Hammond, ed., *Review of Research in Education* 20:129–78.

Spagat, Michael. 1994. "Human Capital and Long-Run Growth in Russia." Brown University, Department of Economics, Providence, R.I.

Steller, Arthur W. 1988. *Effective Schools Research: Practice and Promise.* Fastback 276. Bloomington, Ind.: Kappa Educational Foundation.

Stevenson, David Lee, and David P. Baker. 1991. "State Control of the Curriculum and Classroom Instruction." *Sociology of Education* 64:1–10.

Stromquist, N. P. 1994. "Gender and Education." *International Encyclopedia of Education*, vol. 4. 2d ed. New York: Pergamon Press.

Summers, Anita A., and Amy W. Johnson. 1994. "A Review of the Evidence on the Effects of School-Based Management Plans." Paper prepared for the conference on Improving the Performance of America's Schools: Economic Choices. U.S. National Research Council, Washington, D.C.

Summers, Lawrence H. 1992. "Investing in *All* the People." Policy Research Working Paper Series 905. World Bank, Office of the Vice President and Chief Economist, Washington, D.C.

————. 1994. *Investing in All The People: Educating Women in Developing Countries.* EDI Seminar Paper 45. Washington, D.C.: World Bank.

Tan, Jee-Peng. 1991. "Thailand's Education Sector at a Crossroads: Selected Issues." In "Decision and Change in Thailand: Three Studies in Support of the Seventh Plan." World Bank, Asia Country Department II, Washington, D.C.

Tan, Jee-Peng, and Alain Mingat. 1992. *Education in Asia: A Comparative Study of Cost and Financing.* A World Bank Regional and Sectoral Study. Washington, D.C.

Thomas, Christopher, and Christopher Shaw. 1992. *Issues in the Development of Multigrade Schools.* World Bank Technical Paper 172. Washington, D.C.

Thompson, Ann, M. R. Simonson, and C. Hargrave. 1992. *Educational Technology: A Review of the Research* 81(6):71–81.

Tilak, Jandhyala B. G. 1989. *Education and Its Relation to Economic Growth, Poverty, and Income Distribution: Past Evidence and Further Analysis.* World Bank Discussion Paper 46. Washington, D.C.

————. 1993. "Financing Higher Education in India." *Higher Education* 24(1):43–67.

————. 1994. "On Pricing Higher Education." National Institute of Educational Planning and Administration, New Delhi.

Tilson, Thomas. 1991. "Sustainability in Four Interactive Radio Projects: Bolivia, Honduras, Lesotho and Papua New Guinea." In Marlaine E. Lockheed, John Middleton, and Greta S. Nettleton, eds., "Education Technology: Sustainable and Effective Use." PHREE Background Paper 91/32. World Bank, Education and Social Policy Department, Washington, D.C.

Tsang, Mun. 1993. "Case Studies in Financing Quality Basic Education." Paper prepared for the second meeting of the International Consultative Forum on Education for All, New Delhi. World Bank, Education and Social Policy Department, Washington, D.C.

Tuijnman, A. C., and N. Bottani, eds. 1994. *Making Education Count: Developing and Using International Indicators.* Paris: OECD, Centre for Educational Research and Innovation.

Tuijnman, A. C. and T. N. Postlethwaite, eds. 1994. *Monitoring the Standards of Education.* Oxford: Pergamon Press.

UNDP (United Nations Development Programme)/IMPACT. 1991. *Disability Prevention: A Priority for the 90s.* United Nations International Centre, Vienna.

UNESCO (United Nations Educational, Scientific and Cultural Organization). 1990. *Compendium of Statistics on Illiteracy.* Paris.

————. 1993a. *Trends and Projections of Enrollment by Level of Education, by Age and by Sex, 1960–2025.* Paris.

————. 1993b. *World Education Report 1993.* Paris.

UNICEF (United Nations Children's Fund). 1993. *The Progress of Nations.* New York.

United Nations. 1986. "Education and Fertility: Selected Findings from the World Fertility Survey Data." United Nations Population Division Working Paper ESA/P/WP/96. New York.

————. 1987. "Education and Fertility." In *Fertility Behaviour in the Context of Development: Evidence from the World Fertility Survey.* New York.

Velez, Eduardo, Ernesto Schiefelbein, and Jorge Valenzuela. 1993. "Factors Affecting Achievement in Primary Education: A Review of the Literature for Latin America and the Caribbean." Human Resources Development and Operations Policy Working Paper 2. World Bank, Washington, D.C.

Vlasceanu, Lazar. 1993. "Trends, Developments and Needs of Higher Education Systems of the Central and Eastern European Countries." European Centre for Higher Education, Bucharest.

Walberg, Herbert J. 1991. "Synthesis of Research on Teaching." In Merlin C. Wittrock, ed., *Third Handbook of Research on Teaching.* New York: Macmillan.

Warwick, Donald, and Fernando Reimers. 1992. "Teacher Training in Pakistan: Value Added or Money Wasted?" Paper read at the BRIDGES/IEES Conference on Schooling Effectiveness: Cross National Findings. Harvard Institute for International Development, Cambridge, Mass.

Weale, Martin. 1993. "A Critical Evaluation of Rate of Return Analysis." *Economic Journal* 103 (418):729–37.

Westoff, Charles F. 1992. *Age at Marriage, Age at First Birth, and Fertility in Africa.* World Bank Technical Paper 169. Washington, D.C.

World Bank. 1980. *Education.* Sector Policy Paper. Washington, D.C.

———. 1986. *Financing Education in Developing Countries: An Exploration of Policy Options.* Washington, D.C.

———. 1988. *Education in Sub-Saharan Africa: Policies for Adjustment, Revitalization, and Expansion.* Washington, D.C.

———. 1990a. *Primary Education.* A World Bank Policy Paper. Washington, D.C.

———. 1990b. *World Development Report: Poverty.* New York: Oxford University Press.

———. 1991a. "Republic of Ghana: Community Secondary Schools Construction Project." Staff Appraisal Report 9556-GH. Africa Region, Country Department IV, Washington, D.C.

———. 1991b. "Romania: Accelerating the Transition: Human Resources Strategy for the 1990s." Report 9577-RO. Europe and Central Asia Region, Country Department I, Washington, D.C.

———. 1991c. *Vocational and Technical Education and Training.* A World Bank Policy Paper. Washington, D.C.

———. 1991d. *World Development Report: The Challenge of Development.* New York: Oxford University Press.

———. 1992. "Poland: Reorienting Investments in Human Capital: A Critical Review of Secondary Education and Training Systems." Report 10697-POL. Europe and Central Asia Region, Country Department II, Washington, D.C.

———. 1993a. *The East Asian Miracle: Economic Growth and Public Policy.* A World Bank Policy Research Report. New York: Oxford University Press.

———. 1993b. "Female Secondary School Assistance Project: Bangladesh." Staff Appraisal Report 11386-BD. South Asia Region, Country Department I, Washington, D.C.

———. 1993c. "Indonesia: Public Expenditures, Prices and the Poor." Indonesia Resident Mission Report 11293-ID. East Asia and Pacific Region, Country Department III, Washington, D.C.

————. 1993d. "Secondary Education Project for Colombia." Report 11834-CO. Latin America and the Caribbean Region, Country Department III, Washington, D.C.

————. 1993e. "Venezuela 2000: Education for Growth and Social Equity." Report 11130-VE, Latin America and the Caribbean Region, Country Department I, Washington, D.C.

————. 1993f. *World Development Report: Investing in Health.* New York: Oxford University Press.

————. 1994a. "Colombia Poverty Assessment Report." Draft. Latin America and the Caribbean Region, Country Department III, Washington, D.C.

————. 1994b. *Enhancing Women's Participation in Economic Development.* Washington, D.C.

————. 1994c. *Enriching Lives: Overcoming Vitamin and Mineral Malnutrition in Developing Countries.* Washington, D.C.

————. 1994d. "Guatemala– Basic Education Strategy: Equity and Efficiency in Education." Report 13304-GU. Latin America and the Caribbean Region, Country Department II, Washington, D.C. Available from the World Bank Public Information Center as PIC573.

————. 1994e. *Higher Education: The Lessons of Experience.* Washington, D.C.

————. 1994f. "Kenya Poverty Assessment." Africa Region, Country Department II, Washington, D.C.

————. 1994g. "Kenya Public Expenditure Review." Draft. Africa Region, Country Department II, Washington, D.C.

————. 1994h. The World Bank, *Learning from the Past, Embracing the Future.* Washington, D.C.

————. 1994i. "Mexico: Second Primary Education Project." Report 12529-ME. Latin America and the Caribbean Region, Country Department II, Washington, D.C. Available from the World Bank Public Information Center as PIC 153.

————. 1994j. *Provision for Children with Special Educational Needs in the Asia Region: Some Developments in Current Practice.* World Bank Technical Paper 261. Asia Technical Department, Washington, D.C.

————. 1994k. "Romania: Reform of Higher Education and Research." Europe and Central Asia Region, Country Department I, Washington, D.C.

————. 1994l. "Russia: Education in the Transition." Europe and Central Asia Region, Country Department III, Washington, D.C.

————. 1994m. "Uganda Social Sector Strategy." Report 10765-UG. Africa Region, Country Department II, Washington, D.C.

————. 1994n. *World Development Report: Infrastructure for Development.* New York: Oxford University Press.

————. 1995. *World Development Report 1995: Workers in an Integrating World.* New York: Oxford University Press.

————. Various years. *World Bank Annual Report.* Washington, D.C.

Wu, Kin Bing. 1993. *Mongolia: Financing Education during Economic Transition.* World Bank Discussion Paper 226. Washington, D.C.

Wynne, E. A. 1980. *Looking at Schools: Good, Bad and Indifferent.* Lexington, Mass.: Heath.

Young, Mary Eming. 1994. "Integrated Early Child Development: Challenges and Opportunities." Human Resources Development and Operations Policy Working Paper 40. World Bank, Washington, D.C.

Ziderman, Adrian, and Douglas Albrecht. 1995. *Financing Universities in Developing Countries*. London: Falmer Press.

Other Recent Development in Practice Books

Toward Gender Equality: The Role of Public Policy

Better Urban Services: Finding the Right Incentives
(also available in French and Spanish)

Strengthening the Effectiveness of Aid: Lessons for Donors

*Enriching Lives: Overcoming Vitamin and Mineral Malnutrition
in Developing Countries* (also available in French and Spanish)

A New Agenda for Women's Health and Nutrition (also available in French)

Population and Development: Implications for the World Bank

*East Asia's Trade and Investment: Regional and Global Gains
from Liberalization*

Governance: The World Bank's Experience

Higher Education: The Lessons of Experience (also available in French
and Spanish)

Better Health in Africa: Experience and Lessons Learned (also available
in French)

Argentina's Privatization Program: Experience, Issues, and Lessons

Sustaining Rapid Development in East Asia and the Pacific